CECIL J. ALLEN

SALUTE TO THE
LMS

LONDON
IAN ALLAN

First published 1972

SBN 7110 0256 8

© Ian Allan 1972

*Published by Ian Allan Ltd, Shepperton, Surrey, and printed in Great Britain
by Morrison and Gibb Ltd, London and Edinburgh*

Contents

Cover and centre page painting: Streamlined
Pacific No. 6243 *City of Lancaster* passes Edge Hill
with a Liverpool–London express.
[from a painting by J. L. Chapman

1 · *Strange Bedfellows*

ADVERSITY, the old proverb tells us, can bring together some strange bedfellows. This is certainly how the adversity of World War I affected some of the railways of Britain. After the war the vast increases in the cost of labour and materials would have landed a number of the individual companies in bankruptcy, and the Government regarded it as unavoidable that all the railways should be merged into a few large groups. This was in order that the stronger companies should be able to come to the support of the weaker, and that by amalgamations on a large scale administrative and operating costs should be substantially reduced. During the war the Government had assumed control of the railways; a little less than three years after the Armistice the Royal Assent was given, on August 19, 1921, to a Bill compelling all the railways of Great Britain, with a few minor exceptions, to form themselves into four large grouped companies.

Now with some of the new companies this compulsory grouping gave no great difficulties. In particular, the Great Western Railway had little more to do than to absorb a number of minor railways in Wales and to remain the Great Western, with all its traditional practices, its reputation and its *esprit de corps* unchanged. In the London & North Eastern group were three companies—the Great Northern, the Great Central and the Great Eastern—which had attempted in 1909 to amalgamate, but were forbidden leave by the same capricious Mother of Parliaments that twelve years later was now compelling them to join forces. The other chief constituents of the LNER group, the North Eastern and North British Railways, for many years had been partners with the Great Northern in the East Coast Route to Scotland. So, apart from some efforts by the North Eastern, the most influential member of this group, to be the dominant partner, relations in the LNER group were reasonably harmonious from the start.

But in the London Midland & Scottish group it was a different matter. Between its two principal constituents, the London & North Western and Midland railways, there had never been much love lost. They had always been strong competitors,

both on land, and, with the traffic to and from Ireland, at sea. Their administrative and operating methods differed considerably, as did their motive power; and between their great locomotive works—those of the LNWR at Crewe and of the Midland at Derby—relations were not going to be of the happiest for some time to come.

Each railway had a Scottish partner; the LNWR was allied with the Caledonian Railway, the two forming the West Coast Route, while the Midland was associated with both the Glasgow & South Western and the North British Railways. Had the Scottish lines been formed into a group of their own, it would have been another case of "strange bedfellows", with the highly antagonistic Caledonian and North British lines thus thrown together, but in any event such a grouping would not have been financially viable. So it was that the North British and the Great North of Scotland lines went into the LNER group, and the Caledonian, Glasgow & South Western and Highland into the LMSR, the Scottish lines willy-nilly to be under a measure of dominance from England.

But it was chiefly the relations between the London & North Western and Midland constituents—"strange bedfellows" indeed—which were to determine the future of the London Midland & Scottish Railway. It took quite a few out of the twenty-five years' history of that company for all the internal differences to be resolved, and this was chiefly, as we shall see later, as the result of bringing into the administration some men of outstanding character from outside.

We have first to consider briefly the origin and development of the principal constituents of the LMSR group. The London & North Western Railway, which proudly accepted from its admirers the title "The Premier Line", and claimed to be "the biggest joint stock corporation in the world", with an authorised capital of £124m, was certainly the most influential constituent. The first section of its most important main line, that out of Euston terminus in London, had been opened in stages through Rugby to Birmingham in 1837 and 1838, but its completion had been forestalled in 1837 by that of the Grand Junction Railway, from Birmingham to Crewe and Warrington, with connections to both Manchester and Liverpool. Joining the two latter cities was the historic Liverpool & Manchester Railway, opened as far back as 1830; a short length of this line was used

◀ An impressive view of a Royal Scot—No. 6143 *The South Staffordshire Regiment* rounds the curve from Edge Hill, Liverpool, to the south with an express to Euston.   [Eric Treacy

when the main line from London was extended by the North Union Railway from Warrington to Preston, but was later dispensed with when the short cut-off was completed between Winwick and Golborne Junctions.

In July, 1846, there came the incorporation of the London & North Western Railway, bringing all the foregoing lines under a common ownership, together with extensions of the North Union from Preston to Fleetwood and Lancaster. By the end of that year the Lancaster & Carlisle Railway, soon to be absorbed by the LNWR, had come into being, and also the direct Trent Valley line from Rugby to Stafford via Tamworth and Lichfield, completed just after the LNWR incorporation.

Incidentally, these successive railway openings by what had been independent companies explain what may seem to the observant traveller today to be a mystery of mileposting. On the way to the Border by a London Midland Region express, he will note one continuous series of mileposts as far as Golborne Junction, just north of Warrington, where he will see milepost 1 of a new series which has started from Parkside Junction, on the former Liverpool & Manchester Railway, and extends to Preston. Here begins a third series, beginning at zero and extending to Lancaster, while a fourth series covers the length of the former Lancaster & Carlisle line, completing the 299 miles from Euston.

By 1848 the important North Wales main line had been brought into use as far as Bangor, but two years were to elapse before Robert Stephenson's great task of crossing the Menai Straits by his Britannia Tubular Bridge had provided rail access to Anglesey and the port of Holyhead. Of the remaining main lines the one of most note was that which extended the Liverpool & Manchester line eastwards through the Pennines by way of Standedge Tunnel to Huddersfield and Leeds, there to connect with the North Eastern Railway and provide a highway from Lancashire to Hull, Newcastle and the North-East Coast. Joint with the Great Western Railway was the line southwards along the Welsh Borders from Shrewsbury to Hereford, from there giving access over GWR metals to the London & North Western's completely isolated lines in the valleys of South Wales; there was also the lonely single-track route from Craven Arms through the Welsh spas to Swansea.

In the last year of its independent existence, 1922, the London & North Western Railway amalgamated with the Lancashire & Yorkshire

▲ Reminder of 1837—Euston's famous Doric Arch, which remained *in situ* until the station reconstruction began in the 1960s.   [British Railways

Railway, with which it had always had friendly relations, no doubt with an eye to keeping or trying to keep the Midland in its place after the grouping! The L&Y covered large areas of the counties named in its title with a complicated network of lines, mostly very steeply graded, which it worked with a quiet efficiency.

The nucleus of the Midland Railway, up to the grouping the third largest independent railway system in Great Britain, was a small 16-mile line from Leicester to Swannington, which included the mile-long Glenfield Tunnel, opened in 1832. But the main constituents of the MR were three separate railways of considerably greater importance—the Midland Counties, the Birmingham & Derby, and the North Midland. The Midland Counties was opened in stages during 1839 and 1840 from Rugby, where it connected with the London & Birmingham, to Leicester and Trent, from which junction it forked into lines to Derby and Nottingham. The year 1840 saw the completion of the North Midland line from Derby through Masborough and Normanton to Leeds, with a branch, opened two years earlier, from Masborough into Sheffield. Then there was the Birmingham & Derby, built southwards through Burton and Tamworth originally to a junction with the London

▲ Euston's Great Hall, which also disappeared in the reconstruction. George Stephenson gazes benignly down from his pedestal. The galleries led to the former LNW Head Offices.　　　　　[BR

▼ Platforms 1 and 2 on the arrival side of the old Euston, showing the curve of the roof.　　　　　[BR

▲ Grandest of all London's terminals—Sir Gilbert Scott's Gothic frontage to the Midland Railway's St. Pancras Station, still in existence, though offices have replaced the former hotel.   [BR

▼ The 240 ft. clear span of Barlow's St. Pancras roof, the ties of which are beneath the platforms.   [BR

▲ The approach to St. Pancras, with LMS Class 5 4-6-0 No. 44984 heading a Manchester express out of the station. The former St. Pancras Goods Station to the right. [BR

▼ New Street Station, Birmingham, in former days— the London & North Western platforms, looking north. The Midland platforms were well to the left. [BR

& Birmingham at Hampton-in-Arden; this was completed in 1839, but was supplemented with a direct spur from Whitacre into Birmingham, brought into use three years later. It was in 1844 that these three railways were linked up by the incorporation of the Midland Railway, which purchased the Leicester & Swannington line in 1845.

In its earlier years the relations of the Midland Railway with the London & North Western were reasonably good. Passenger traffic from London to the North-East of England left Euston station of the LNWR and was hauled by that company to Rugby, where the MR took over, continuing via Leicester, Derby, and Masborough to Normanton; there the trains were handed over to the York & North Midland. All was well while the Midland Railway remained within the territory indicated by its name. But it was a different matter when this expanding company made plans to break out in various directions and engage in enterprises which were likely to prove highly competitive with the services of its neighbours.

The first such was when, in the year of its

incorporation, the Midland stepped in and under the nose of the Great Western Railway bought up both the Birmingham & Gloucester and Bristol & Gloucester Railways, so securing a foothold in the heart of GWR territory and a route which from then to the present day has always been the most direct and the fastest from the Midlands to the West of England. By 1846 the Midland had stretched out eastwards from Nottingham to Lincoln; and when four years later the Great Northern main line was opened through Newark, crossing the MR Lincoln line on the level just north of the town, it was the MR, the first in the field, that controlled the signalling of the crossing from that time onwards.

Next the Midland management began to cast envious eyes on Manchester. Its first step in this direction was a branch from Ambergate through Matlock to Rowsley, built jointly with the London & North Western because it gave access at Cromford to the latter's High Peak line. But the latter might well have hesitated had it realised that this would be the first instalment of a Midland main line to Manchester, which the LNWR violently

opposed. Owing to the engineering difficulties of carrying the line through the mountainous Peak District, and other complications, however, it was not until 1867 that the first Midland trains were seen in Manchester.

Meantime there had come the most challenging move of all. The Midland management decided, in the 1850s, that the time had come for its system to be linked by its own main line with London. So it obtained powers to build a new line southwards from Leicester through Kettering and Wellingborough to Bedford, and from there to a junction with the newly opened Great Northern line at Hitchin, the powers including the right to continue over the GNR into Kings Cross. So it was that Midland trains for the first time made their way into London in 1858.

For both the railways concerned, however, this proved anything but a successful move; the 32 miles of GN line became hopelessly congested, and with the Midland trains, needless to say, always having to give preference to those of the owning company. In this matter, incidentally, the Great Northern was getting its own back on the Midland for what had happened in 1852 at Nottingham, where the first GNR train into that city, using Midland metals with the help of running powers, had its locomotive impounded by Midland men and kept a prisoner for several weeks thereafter!

Be that as it may, by the 1860s the Midland management had been forced to the conclusion that it must have its own independent line into the capital. So the expensive task was faced of extending from Bedford through Luton and St. Albans to a London terminus next door to the one which the MR had been using up till then. Such was the genesis of St. Pancras, with its opulent hotel and the splendour of its Gothic frontage, which it owed jointly to Sir Gilbert Scott, the architect, and W. H. Barlow, the engineer of the London extension. From 1868, therefore, the formerly provincial Midland Railway had obtained its own foothold in London, though its principal activities continued to be concentrated at Derby.

Meantime the Midland had been casting covetous eyes in other directions also, and particularly on the possibility of securing a share of the lucrative Anglo-Scottish traffic. From 1852 the MR had been working the so-called "Little North Western" line from Skipton to Lancaster and Carnforth, while a branch from Lancashire's Clapham Junction to Ingleton made an end-on junction there with a branch of the LNWR from

▲ Olive Mount rock cutting, at the approach to Liverpool from the Manchester direction, first blasted out for the Liverpool & Manchester Railway.
[BR

Low Gill, on the West Coast main line. This was the way that Midland passengers to Scotland had to take, but the rival line was far from disposed to give any assistance to these passengers, who received such scandalous treatment that once again the MR was faced with the prospect of obtaining an independent route, in this case to Carlisle. So it was that in 1865 the MR received Parliamentary sanction to build its own Settle & Carlisle line through the mountains of Westmorland. So high was the estimated cost of the plan, however, coming so soon after the costly extension to St. Pancras, that for a time the Midland was inclined to back out of the project, but pressure from its future Scottish allies, the Glasgow & South Western and North British Railways, was so strong that in 1869 work was begun, and in 1876 the first through trains were run from St. Pancras to both Glasgow St. Enoch and Edinburgh Waverley, using the Settle & Carlisle line.

And what was the next activity of this restless company? It concerned the great city of Bradford, which up to the first decade of the century had always been at the end of branches of the three railways serving it. The Midland therefore conceived the idea of carrying a main line to the north right through Bradford, even though trains using this route would not be able to serve Leeds also. So, in 1909, there came about the opening of the Royston & Thornhill Railway, leaving the Midland main line to Leeds at Royston, just north of Cudworth, and cutting across to join the Lancashire & Yorkshire main Wakefield-Manchester line at Thornhill. Just short of this junction the proposed Bradford line branched off to the north and got as far as Dewsbury; while four miles to the west another branch was thrown off, this time from Mirfield into Huddersfield. The continuation from Dewsbury through Bradford to Shipley would have involved a good deal of tunnelling, and would have been extremely costly; this time the Midland really did get cold feet, and with the abandonment of the Dewsbury-Bradford section Bradford never got its through main line after all. Limited use was made from then on of the Royston-Thornhill line and its branches, but not enough to justify what had been spent on its construction.

There was one more extension of the Midland system which was certainly not likely to make the MR popular with the management immediately affected. The Great Eastern Railway had always been anxious to acquire, if possible, the inde-

▼ How the Midland obtained its independent route to Carlisle—the Settle & Carlisle main line crossing Ribblehead Viaduct, in the wilds of Westmorland, with Ingleborough as an impressive background.
[John Goss

pendent London Tilbury & Southend Railway, which occupied what might well have been regarded as GER territory, along the north shore of the Thames estuary. The difficulty was that such an acquisition would have involved the GER in paying LT&SR shareholders a higher dividend than it was able to afford to its own proprietors. Suddenly the Great Eastern authorities learned that Sir Guy Granet, the astute Midland General Manager, had taken over the LT&SR, lock, stock and barrel, and that Midland control would begin from January 1, 1912. So the lucrative commuter traffic between London, Leigh-on-Sea, Westcliff and Southend, by the shortest route, passed into Midland hands, and, still worse from the GER point of view, the important port of Tilbury.

Thus it was that by the time of the grouping the tentacles of the Midland Railway extended from Carlisle in the north to Bristol and Bath in the south (and with the help of the Somerset & Dorset Joint Line as far as the south coast at Bournemouth); to Hereford and Swansea in the west; to Southend-on-Sea and Lincoln in the east; and with the help of another joint line, the Swinton & Knottingley, nearly to York in the north-east—a most comprehensive and influential network. And further, as described in Chapter 14, the Midland controlled in Ireland the lines of the Northern Counties Committee from Larne and Belfast to Londonderry, and jointly those of the County Donegal Joint Committee as far west as the Atlantic Coast at Killybegs.

2 · The Other LMSR Constituent Companies

IN SCOTLAND the biggest and most important constituent of the London Midland & Scottish group was the Caledonian Railway. In the 1840s an agreement was reached by this Scottish company with the London & North Western Railway to build a joint station at Carlisle, out of which the first section of the Caledonian, as far as to Beattock, was opened in 1847. For a year passengers for Glasgow and Edinburgh were carried forward from Beattock by coach, but in 1848 the West Coast main line was completed throughout from London to the two Scottish cities. Scotland in those early years had already acquired a number of minor railways, parts of no fewer than eleven of which were used in connecting Carlisle with Perth and Aberdeen.

One very odd result of this medley of lines was that just north of Coatbridge the Caledonian trains had to pass from Gartsherrie to Garnqueen South Junction over ¾ mile of the former Monkland & Kirkintilloch Railway, which eventually passed into the hands of the Caledonian's traditional enemy, the North British, and matters so remained right on to LMSR and LNER days. However, the Caledonian had a more than ample revenge in that North British trains were unable to reach Aberdeen without travelling over 38 miles of the Caledonian main line from Kinnaber Junction onwards. The same thing happened in reverse when in 1865, after years of unfriendly negotiation, the North British had secured control of the highly strategic direct line from Edinburgh to Glasgow, over which, with its loop through Falkirk Grahamston, Caledonian trains from Edinburgh to Perth and beyond always had to pass before reaching their own system at Larbert.

In 1848 the Scottish Central Railway made its way into Perth and in the same year the Scottish Midland got as far as Forfar; two years later the Arbroath & Forfar and Aberdeen Railways had completed the line from Forfar into the Granite City. All were absorbed by the Caledonian Railway in 1865. The lengthy branch from Dunblane through Callander to Oban, completed after many vicissitudes in 1880, was worked by the Caledonian, but this Callander & Oban line remained an independent company till the end of Caledonian history.

Except in the environs of Glasgow, and down the Clyde, the Glasgow & South Western Railway had the south-west corner of Scotland virtually to itself. Actually a short section of its system, from Kilmarnock to Troon, was the first railway in Scotland, but during its early years this was operated by horses. The first opening of a line in this area with steam traction was in 1840, from Glasgow to Ayr, under the title of Glasgow, Paisley, Kilmarnock & Ayr Railway. It was after the completion in 1850 of the main line from Kilmarnock to Dumfries and on to a junction with the Caledonian at Gretna that the title of Glasgow & South Western Railway was assumed.

The original G&SW main line to the south passed through Paisley; in 1873, jointly with the Caledonian, the more direct but steeply graded line through Barrhead to Kilmarnock was brought into use. For some years Bridge Street, on the south side of the River Clyde, was the Glasgow terminus of the G&SWR, and it is from Bridge Street that the mileposts are measured; the transfer to St. Enoch took place in 1876. The same year saw the completion of the important line from Ayr through Girvan to Stranraer, joining at Challoch Junction the Portpatrick & Wigtownshire Joint line from Dumfries.

The inception of the Highland Railway recalls one of the bitterest struggles in British railway history. It was, in effect, between the cities of

Inverness and Aberdeen, the latter's interests dominated by the Great North of Scotland Railway. When in 1846 a Bill was presented to Parliament for a Perth & Inverness Railway, it was thrown out, largely because our legislators thought that the gradients through the mountains would be too severe; but it was significant that in the same session the GNSR was authorised to build its proposed line from Aberdeen to Huntly. After seven years Inverness decided to make a more modest start, and though opposed by the GNSR managed to get Parliamentary approval for a 15½-mile line from Inverness to Nairn. Next followed a temporary *rapprochement* with the Great North, and the incorporation of the joint Inverness & Aberdeen Junction Railway, to continue from Nairn through Forres and Elgin to Keith, there linking up with the Huntly-Keith extension of the GNSR from Aberdeen, which was opened in 1858.

But some rather underhand proceedings by the GNSR resulted in the dissolution of the partnership, and a strengthening of the determination of Inverness to have its own direct main line to the south. So it was that in 1860, with strong public support, the Inverness & Perth Junction Railway was formed, and this time obtained Parliamentary sanction with its 1861 Act of Incorporation. An able engineer named Joseph Mitchell did the planning and his company carried out the work; the line was opened for traffic in September, 1863.

It branched from the Inverness & Aberdeen Junction line at Forres, and climbed over 1,052 ft. altitude on Dava Moor to reach Aviemore, in the Spey Valley, and later over 1,484 ft.—Britain's highest railway summit—at Druimuachdar before descending to Blair Atholl, Pitlochry and Dunkeld; here it joined a short line which some years before had been built from a junction at Stanley with the Caledonian main line from Perth to Aberdeen. In the same year the Inverness & Perth and Inverness & Aberdeen lines (the latter terminating

at Keith) were amalgamated to form the Highland Railway.

In 1898 the circuit through Forres was made unnecessary by the opening of the direct line from Aviemore to Inverness, which shortened the distance by 34 miles and made possible some considerable accelerations; but this was at the cost of steepening the ruling gradient from 1 in 70 to 1 in 60. The long continuous gradients did not give the difficulty in operation that had been feared, but a worse handicap was snow in winter over the exposed high level stretches of the line. Before the opening of the original Inverness & Perth Railway a start had been made also with railway communication north of Inverness, to Dingwall in 1862; it was 1871, however, before Helmsdale was reached, and three years later that Highland trains for the first time ran into Wick and Thurso. Not until 1897, after having terminated for 27 years at Strome Ferry, was the lengthy Dingwall & Skye line opened throughout to the Kyle of Lochalsh, three years, incidentally, after the West Highland line of the North British had reached Fort William.

The remaining LMSR constituents were all

◀ Dalston Junction of the North London Railway, which became a subsidiary of the LNWR in 1908.
[R. L. Coles

▶ Furthest north on the LMSR, Wick Station of the former Highland Railway, 730 miles from Euston.
[K. L. Cook

▶ Furthest south of the LMSR system—Bath Green Park Station of the former Midland Railway, also the western terminus of the Somerset & Dorset Joint Railway.   [M. C. Burdge

smaller companies. The most historic was the Maryport & Carlisle, incorporated as far back as 1837 for a line round the Cumberland coast from Carlisle to the coal and iron districts of Maryport, Workington and Whitehaven, and distinguished by paying to its proprietors, for some years after its opening in 1845, a dividend of no less than 13 per cent. A year later the first section of the Furness Railway had been brought into use, but the main line, throughout from Whitehaven to a junction with the London & North Western Railway at Carnforth, was not completed until some years later.

At first passengers from the south for the important town of Barrow had to travel to Askham, and from there by branch train, but in 1882 a new loop line was opened from Dalton to Askham which, though it increased the length of the main line by 7½ miles, brought passengers more expeditiously into a fine new station in the heart of the town. The Barrow loop is but one of the circuits made by this extremely sinuous line; in 1865 plans were made to cut out another wide circuit by a lengthy bridge across the Duddon estuary, but these came to nothing. The mainstay of Furness traffic was hematite iron ore, iron and steel and coal; one reminder that ore can cause casualties as well as profits was when a Furness locomotive suddenly subsided into an ore working at Lindal, and was never recovered.

Last we have the prosperous North Staffordshire Railway, occupying a strategic position in the heart of London & North Western and Midland

territory. Based on Stoke-on-Trent, the North Stafford owned the direct route between the LNWR and Midland centres of Crewe and Derby respectively; also with its line from Macclesfield through Stoke to Colwich it provided the LNWR with the shortest route between Manchester and London, used daily by certain expresses, in particular in LMSR days the southbound "Lancastrian" and the northbound "Mancunian". For this reason, after nationalisation the Colwich-Stoke-Macclesfield-Cheadle Hulme line shared with the main line via Crewe the benefits of electrification.

Certain important joint lines remained joint property after the formation of the London Midland & Scottish Railway, though by agreement one only of the partners became responsible for their motive power, rolling stock and operation. In the Cheshire Lines the LMSR retained a one-third share only; the LNER had two shares, as the previous ownership had been between the Midland, Great Central and Great Northern Railways. The Midland & Great Northern Joint Railway, which had given the Midland access to Kings Lynn and the Norfolk Coast round from Sheringham to Lowestoft, became LMSR and LNER in equal shares, as did the Somerset & Dorset Joint Line equally between the LMSR and the Southern. Finally, the important cross-country route from Shrewsbury to Hereford passed jointly into the hands of the London Midland & Scottish and Great Western Railways.

Such was the amalgam that in 1923 produced the London Midland & Scottish Railway, destined to

◀ Nearing Britain's highest railway summit—Dalnaspidal Station, at the approach to the 1,484 ft. of Druimuachdar. Ex-Highland 4-6-0 No. 14764 heads a train of North British, Midland, West Coast and Highland stock. [BR

▼ The sharply curved approach to St. Enoch Station in Glasgow of the former Glasgow & South Western Railway, with a train leaving for Ayr. [Derek Cross

have a life of precisely a quarter of a century. With the two "strange bedfellows" that have been the subject of Chapter 1 in the dominant position, and the Scottish lines far from happy at control from south of the Border, the start of the new group was not of the most auspicious character. Seniority rather than outstanding ability marked most of the initial administrative appointments, and it was not until some years later that two men of strong character were brought in from outside, and by their influence helped to achieve the transformation that raised the LMSR to the position of high prestige that it occupied before the outbreak of war in 1939.

One was the economist Josiah Stamp, appointed in 1926 to the entirely new post of President of the Executive, and in the following year assuming the Chairmanship of the Company. The other, in 1932 taking the office of Chief Mechanical Engineer, was W. A. Stanier. Both in due course deservedly received the honour of knighthood for their services to their railways and to their country. It is only sad to have to add that Sir Josiah Stamp's Presidency was suddenly terminated during World War II by the German bomb that demolished his house at Shortlands.

▲ Caledonian station artistry—the exterior of Wemyss Bay Station on the Clyde, still unchanged in modern times.   [BR

▲ Scottish outpost in the far North-West—ex-Highland 5 ft. 3 in. 4-6-0 No. 57956 shunting at Kyle of Lochalsh, the port for Skye.   [W. J. V. Anderson

3 · The Way and Works

IF THERE WAS one realm of engineering more than another in which the London Midland & Scottish Railway had the ascendancy over the other three groups, it was tunnelling. Five of the nine British tunnels over 2 miles in length, and 24 out of the 55 that were more than a mile long, were on the LMSR. Exactly half the latter were contributed by the Midland Railway, including Totley, 3 miles 950 yd., second only in length to the Great Western's Severn Tunnel. In the latter part of World War II the 10 am train from St. Pancras, by which I had frequently to travel—wartime version of the "Thames-Clyde Express"—and which pursued a circuitous course via Nottingham and Derby to Sheffield and beyond, travelled through more tunnels than any other train in British history; they included Haverstock Hill, Corby, Glaston, Clay Cross, Bradway and Blea Moor, all over a mile long, and other shorter tunnels in England and Scotland to a grand total of no fewer than 35. Among the London & North Western tunnels was Standedge, 3 miles 60 yd., third longest in Great Britain and actually three tunnels, one double line and two single line. There was also Kilsby, 1 mile 666 yd., part of the former London & Birmingham Railway, opened for traffic in 1837 and the first tunnel of such a length to be completed in this country.

While the LMSR never possessed any bridge on the same scale as the Forth Bridge, on the other side of the country, it could boast several bridge structures of note. Foremost among them was the Britannia Tubular Bridge, the highly original design evolved by Robert Stephenson to carry the main line to Holyhead across the Menai Strait from North Wales into Anglesey. Little could anyone have foreseen that these two rectangular tubes of wrought iron, one for each track and 4,680 tons in weight, would remain in use for 120 years, with their timber linings exposed to risk from the sparks of steam locomotives, until in the diesel age in 1970 it was a careless boy trespasser looking for birds' nests with a naked light that set the timber on fire and virtually destroyed Stephenson's handiwork. The replacement, brought into use in 1972, has a very different appearance.

In Scotland a notable cantilever bridge, with a span of 500 ft., was thrown across the narrow entrance to Loch Etive, at Connel Ferry, to carry the Ballachulish branch of the Callander & Oban Railway; but with the abandonment of the branch in recent years the bridge now carries a road only. At Runcorn the massive steel viaduct carrying the Liverpool main line across the Manchester Ship Canal and the River Mersey remains in use to this day, though now dwarfed by the great steel arch alongside it carrying the main road. The former Glasgow & South Western Railway had the distinction of owning the biggest masonry span in Great Britain and very possibly in the world— Ballochmyle Viaduct, just south of Kilmarnock, with a central arch clearing 181 ft. Of masonry viaducts among the various constituent companies many might be cited; one of particular note was Lockwood Viaduct of the one-time Lancashire & Yorkshire Railway, in the suburbs of Huddersfield on the branch to Penistone, with its 36 spans having a maximum height of 129 ft., and a length of 1,407 ft. In Scotland there is the great curved viaduct carrying the Highland main line across Culloden Moor, with its 29 50-ft. arches, up to 130 ft. high, and overall length of 1,785 ft.

When it comes to track, one of the boasts of the London & North Western Railway was that it possessed "the best permanent way in the world". One ground for this bold claim was that it was the first railway in Britain to lay rails 60 ft. in length, produced in its own rolling mill at Crewe Works, where an equally proud boast was that everything needed by a railway was made from locomotives to wooden legs for any of the staff that had lost theirs in an accident. In the early thirties I was sent by my railway to Crewe to enquire whether rail rolling by the railway itself could compare in cost with buying rails from outside, and having seen for myself the use of small ingots no bigger than sufficient each to produce a single 60-ft. rail, which after cropping resulted in an excessive amount of waste, I was compelled to report to the contrary. It was therefore little surprise to me that in 1933, the year after he was appointed Chief Mechanical Engineer of the LMSR, Stanier closed down and dismantled the Crewe rail mill.

While the LNWR used 60-ft. rails, the Midland specialised in rails 36 ft. in length, and the Caledonian in an unusual 32-ft. length. The Midland was the only railway in Britain to lay bull-head rails as heavy as 100 lb. to the yd.; even into LMSR days main lines were not going beyond 95 lb. per yd. As to length, by LMSR days 45-ft. rails were in general use, but by the end of LMSR history 60 ft. had become the general standard. To the Engineering Department of the LMSR goes the credit of having been the first British railway to realise that in the controversy of bull-head *versus* flat-bottom rails it was hardly possible for Britain to be right and almost all the rest of the world wrong; so it was that the LMSR was the first in this country to lay in flat-bottom rails, weighing 110 lb. per yd. The result was a foregone conclusion; the LNER soon followed suit, and flat-bottom track is now the British standard.

Apart from the Snowdon Mountain Tramway, the LMSR could claim the most lofty stretch of line in Great Britain, at an altitude of 1,484 ft. in the Druimuachdar or Drumochter Pass, on the Highland main line between Blair Atholl and Kingussie. A little further north, beyond Aviemore, was Slochd Mhuic, 1,315 ft. In former days the Caledonian Railway had a summit level between these two, of 1,405 ft. at Leadhills, on the lonely branch between Elvanfoot and Wanlockhead, but this branch was abandoned many years ago. The West Coast main line, of course, has always had its two famous summits, south and north of the Border, Shap, 915 ft., on the former LNWR, and Beattock, 1,014 ft., on the former Caledonian; but both were beaten by the Midland Settle & Carlisle line, which in the Westmorland hills topped 1,167 ft. at Ais Gill. The toilsome approach grades to these summits have not exceeded 1 in 100 up to Ais Gill, but the southern approach to Shap steepens to 1 in 75, that to Beattock for 10 miles averages 1 in 70, and that from Inverness southwards to Slochd Mhuic at first climbs for some miles at 1 in 60.

As the first track water-troughs in Britain were those laid down by John Ramsbottom of the London & North Western Railway in 1859, it was quite appropriate that the total number of LMSR troughs, 35 in all, considerably exceeded those owned by any other British railway. The very first, on the North Wales main line near Aber, eventually had increased to four on the 102½ miles between Crewe and Holyhead alone; while beween Euston and Glasgow Pacific No. 6201 *Princess Elizabeth*, on the record non-stop runs of November 1936, had no fewer than eleven chances of taking water *en route*. The second biggest contribution in the LMSR group was made by the Lancashire & Yorkshire Railway, with ten track-trough installations; even the LYR passenger tank engines were fitted with scoops designed to take water in either direction of running. The troughs laid down by the Midland Railway on the Settle & Carlisle line near Dent, at more than 1,000 ft. above sea level, were at the highest altitude of any in Britain, and the oddest location of any British troughs was *inside* Standedge Tunnel of the LNWR, at the western end, as this was the only available stretch of level line between Huddersfield and Manchester.

The comprehensive term "Way and Works" of course includes stations, and of notable structures the LMSR possessed a great variety. Pride of place, probably, must go to the London terminus of the Midland Railway, at St. Pancras, with its highly ornate Gothic frontage. The span of the immense all-over roof, 210 ft., has always created a record for Great Britain; the roof-ties are below the station floor, and below that has been a vast storage for the products of Burton-on-Trent, in the planning of which a beer barrel was the most important unit of measurement. With the spacious Euston of today it is difficult to realise how inconvenient the former Euston of the London & Birmingham Railway, in later years extended by the London & North Western, had become. In the centre was Stephenson's Great Hall, separating

▲ Runcorn Bridge, carrying the LNWR main line from Euston to Liverpool across the River Mersey.   [BR

▼ A Lancashire & Yorkshire viaduct of note—Lockwood, on the line from Huddersfield to Penistone, with its 36 masonry spans and maximum height of 126 ft.   [Kenneth Field

◄ Robert Stephenson's Britannia Tubular Bridge, from the Anglesey side. A photograph taken a few days before the disastrous fire that has compelled a complete reconstruction.   [C. N. Kneale

▼ Britain's biggest masonry arch—Ballochmyle Viaduct, on the former Glasgow & South Western main line south of Kilmarnock, with its clear span of 181 ft.   [Derek Cross

the old terminus from the later departure platforms 12 to 15 inclusive, and with other odd platforms in between; in front of the station was the famous Doric Arch, which with the Great Hall disappeared in the modern reconstruction.

In Scotland the Caledonian Railway brought some fine stations into the LMSR group, particularly the Central Station in Glasgow; and one of the most attractive stations in the whole country is the ex-Caledonian Wemyss Bay, on the Clyde. It is a curious fact that whereas the station hotels at Euston, St. Pancras, and New Street (Birmingham) have all now ceased to exist, though the stations themselves remain, at St. Enoch, Glasgow (the former Glasgow & South Western terminus) and Princes Street, Edinburgh, it is the hotels that remain whereas the stations have been closed.

In Manchester the former LNWR Exchange Station had the distinction of being joined to the adjacent Victoria Station of the Lancashire & Yorkshire Railway by the longest continuous railway platform in Britain, 2,194 ft. of it: Exchange

◀ In the Highlands—the viaduct across the Findhorn Valley, near Tomatin, on the Aviemore-Inverness direct line.   [Brian Stephenson

▼ Linslade tunnels, Leighton Buzzard, on the main Euston–Crewe line, with Patriot 4-6-0 No. 5524 *Blackpool* heading a down express.   [W. S. Garth

is now no more. The combined station had 22 platforms and covered 23 acres. New Street, Birmingham, formerly consisted of two completely independent sections, the LNWR on one side and the Midland on the other of a central roadway, with 15 platforms in all; but here, as at Euston, a cramped and inconvenient interior has now been swept away in a comprehensive reconstruction. The same thing has happened at Leeds, where the former cramped Midland Wellington station has now been merged by rebuilding with the adjacent joint New Station of the former London & North Western and North Eastern Companies.

Many other stations of note might be mentioned. Crewe has always been the nerve centre of the Western Lines and Derby of the Midland Lines; Crewe boasts 16 platforms and covers 23 acres. Carlisle, meeting-point of the LNW and Caledonian Railways, and jointly owned by both, up to the grouping had the distinction of welcoming the trains of five other companies—the Midland, North Eastern, North British, Glasgow & South Western and Maryport & Carlisle Railways—the most variegated assortment of locomotive and coach colours seen in any British station with the possible exception of York. Perth and Aberdeen General, the latter jointly owned with the Great North of Scotland Railway and after the grouping joint LMSR and LNER property, were among those possessing main platforms of exceptional length, 1,714 ft. and 1,596 ft. respectively.

▲ Tring Cutting, a major work of excavation through the Chilterns on the London & Birmingham Railway. [BR

▼ Through the Pennines—the impressive eastern end of the three Standedge tunnels, just over 3 miles long, on the former LNWR main line from Manchester to Leeds. [M. Dunnett

4 · *Anglo-Scottish Rivalry — West Coast v East Coast*

FEW IF ANY other warfares in British railway history have been so fierce and so long-continued as that between the West and East Coast Routes for the traffic from London to Scotland. In order to trace its development in London Midland & Scottish days we need to go back to the final years of the last century to recall the almost unbelievable excitements of the "Races" of 1888 and 1895. During the 1880s competition was building up. Since 1870 the East Coast's "Special Scotch Express", in later years to become the "Flying Scotsman", had been leaving Kings Cross for Edinburgh at 10 am, while its rival, many years later to become the "Royal Scot", was departing from Euston at the same hour, and serving both Edinburgh and Glasgow. Both excluded the humble third class passenger from their distinguished interiors.

Suddenly the competition flared up with the announcement by the East Coast companies, in November 1887, that from then on their "Special Scotch Express" would carry passengers of all three classes, and as a result very soon the West Coast lines were beginning to see some of their lucrative traffic draining away to their rivals. So also was the Midland Railway, which by opening its Settle & Carlisle line in 1876 had also obtained direct access, with the help of the North British, to Edinburgh. Up till then the London & North Western Railway had shown little interest in speed, and it therefore came as an electrifying shock when, after keeping their plans a dead secret till the last minute, the West Coast companies announced that from June 2, 1888, their "Day Scotch Express" would have a full hour cut from its times to both Edinburgh and Glasgow, and so would equal the 9-hr. journey time of the East Coast's 10 am from Kings Cross.

The East Coast reply was immediate. No more than a month later it was that their 10 am from Kings Cross would be into Edinburgh at 6.30 pm, 30 minutes ahead of its rival from Euston. So the "Race" was on. It is difficult to imagine staid railway managements scrapping timetables one after another in order to make the fastest times between the English and Scottish capitals, but so it was through the summer of 1888, until on August 7 the West Coast had achieved a time of 7 hr. 38 min. over its 399¾-mile course, while on 31st of the same month the East Coast 10 am from London ran into Edinburgh Waverley at 5.27 pm, in 7 hr. 27 min. from London. In the later stages of the "Race" the times were made by very light first portions of the trains concerned, and official schedules were thrown to the winds; there was only one purpose in view, and that was who could

▲ LNWR Teutonic type Webb 2-2-2-0 compound, Euston–Crewe (1895 Race). [BR

▼ LNWR Precedent type Webb 2-4-0 *Hardwicke*, Crewe–Carlisle (1895 Race). [BR

▲ Caledonian 4-2-2 No. 123 Carlisle–Edinburgh (1888 Race). [P. Ransome-Wallis] ▼ Caledonian 4-4-0 No. 721 *Dunalastair*, Carlisle–Aberdeen (1895 Race). [BR

get there first. But when, at the end of August, by mutual consent the racing came to an end, a permanent benefit had been conferred with the agreement that the time for East Coast day trains between London and Edinburgh should be 8¼ hr., and for those of the West Coast 8½ hr., well below the previous minimum of 9 hr.

But competition had not come to an end; it continued to smoulder, waiting for some move by one side or the other to fan it to a flame once again. This time new and far more exciting racing was prompted by the completion of a great engineering feat—the Forth Bridge—in 1890. Three years earlier Barlow's new bridge over the Firth of Tay had replaced the ill-fated first Tay Bridge, and between them these two bridges had opened up an entirely new route along the East Coast of Scotland; until then an East Coast journey from Edinburgh to Dundee or Aberdeen had involved passengers in ferrying across both firths, an uncomfortable and time-wasting business.

So now the West Coast monopoly of the traffic from London to Perth, Dundee and Aberdeen had come to an end; the East Coast route had become 9½ miles shorter than the West Coast from London to Perth and Inverness, 19 miles shorter to Dundee and 16½ miles shorter to Aberdeen. The only fly in the East Coast ointment was that their trains had to run over 38 miles of Caledonian track from Kinnaber Junction, Montrose, to Aberdeen, and also had to use a short length of Caledonian line into Perth; this gave their rival unlimited chances of holding up the East Coast trains, which from time to time they did not hesitate to do.

Once again a good deal of sparring took place between the two sides from 1890 onwards, with frequent small cuts in train times, but with the East Coast always keeping slightly ahead in both day and night times from London to Dundee and Aberdeen, as well as to Edinburgh. It was a modest West Coast acceleration that precipitated the final crisis. By the beginning of 1895 the arrival in Aberdeen of the 8 pm sleeper from Kings Cross had come down to 7.35 am, while the rival 8 pm from Euston was due 15 min. later. The trivial speed-up was that from June 1, 1895, the West Coast was to cut 10 min. from its schedule, bringing its 8 pm from Euston into Aberdeen 5 min. only behind its counterpart from Kings Cross, at 7.40 am. A month later the latter was accelerated to arrive at 7.20 am, and then came the devastating announcement by the West Coast, on July 15, that from the very next day their 8 pm would reach Aberdeen by 7 am, which it did and with 13 min. to spare!

The "Race to Aberdeen" was now on with a vengeance. Space here does not allow me to go in detail into what happened in the ensuing 37 days, but this has been done in O. S. Nock's fascinating book *The Railway Race to the North*, in which may be read all the amazing written communications and telegrams that passed between the directors and officers of the railways concerned during these hectic weeks. In retrospect it seems almost unbelievable that in their desperate concern to be the "winners", the railway administrations finally cut the racing trains to four-coach and even three-coach formations, and encouraged their drivers to take no notice whatever of scheduled times, but to get there first at all cost, even though this meant taking the most fearsome risks in their negotiation of curves. Anyway, the upshot was that on the night of August 21, 1895, the 8 pm from Kings Cross ran into Aberdeen at 4.40 the following morning—523¼ miles in 520 min. —while on the next day the 8 pm from Euston put in an appearance at 4.32 am—539¾ miles in 512 min.

These record achievements had cut no less than 2 hr. 55 min. and 3 hr. 18 min. from the booked times of the same trains seven weeks before! The sheer lunacy of bringing these night flyers into Aberdeen at between 4 and 5 o'clock in the morning seems to have been little appreciated, and still less that these times were achieved at very considerable risk to the passengers in the two trains. This was to be proved in disastrous fashion a year later, when the 8 pm from Euston was derailed by the drivers of the same double-headed express attempting to take the sharp curve north of Preston station at far too high a speed.

As with the "Race to Edinburgh" of 1888, the night trains to Aberdeen had been accelerated after the 1895 Race, but the Preston accident confirmed the fears of those who had realised the serious risks run in 1895. The upshot was an agreement

▶ Standard formation of the 10 am from Euston in the early part of the century, headed by Caledonian McIntosh 4-6-0 No. 49.   [BR

by all the companies concerned to revert to times much the same as those in operation before the 1895 Race began—an agreement which was to act as a dead hand on all Anglo-Scottish speed for the next 36 years.

And so, to the end of the history of the independent companies, and well into that of the London Midland & Scottish and London & North Eastern Railways, for year after year the 10 am from Euston to Edinburgh and Glasgow and the 10 am from Kings Cross to Edinburgh continued to take 8¼ hr. for their journeys, and in actual running were slower than at the end of the last century, seeing that restaurant cars had made it possible to dispense with or curtail the former lengthy halts for lunch at Preston and York. The principal night trains were faster, taking 8 hr. from Euston to Glasgow and 7¾ hr. from Kings Cross to Edinburgh, but in their case no special meal stops had been necessary. The London-Aberdeen journey still needed 11 hr. 40 min. by the East Coast and 11 hr. 50 min. by the West Coast. Thus it was that after a competitive event without parallel in British railway history there followed more than three decades of inactivity in Anglo-Scottish speed equally without parallel and in this case without justification.

There came, of course, the interruption of World War I, when all Anglo-Scottish services suffered severely. By 1918 the 10 am from Euston was starting at 9.40 and not conveying any London-Glasgow passengers; these had had to transfer to the 8.50 am from St. Pancras. All London-Edinburgh passengers had to use the 10 am from Kings Cross. The only other day train was the 1 pm from Euston, which took 10 hr. 10 min. to reach Glasgow. The Midland managed to run restaurant cars right through to the end of the conflict, though they had long since disappeared from the London & North Western trains. Then followed the period of post-war recovery, and by the time the London Midland & Scottish Railway came into being, at the beginning of 1923, train services in general were once again back to their 1914 standard, or very nearly so.

▶ In later LNWR years. A West Coast Anglo-Scottish express headed by a LNWR Prince of Wales 4-6-0 taking water from Dillicar troughs, near Tebay.

5 · *Anglo-Scottish Rivalry—LMSR v LNER*

FROM NOW ON the competition for Anglo-Scottish traffic was no longer between five railways, but between two only, the LMSR on the West Coast and the LNER on the East Coast. Prestige was at stake, and with combined publicity resources on a scale never known previously in the days of the individual companies. But as the two groups still allowed the wretched 1896 agreement to tie their hands in the matter of speed, for the time being the competitive activities had to take other forms.

One was the provision of more luxurious rolling stock. In the summer of 1908 the West Coast companies had introduced two magnificent trains of 12-wheel coaches on their afternoon Euston-Edinburgh-Glasgow service—the 2 pm from each terminal, in later years to become the "Midday Scot"—and these were still in service. But nothing similar had been done for the 10 am trains in each direction, other than the introduction of restaurant cars, and, on the East Coast, 12-wheel stock of not quite so high a standard of luxury, at the beginning of the century.

So we come to the year 1927. With increasing traffic, the LMSR decided to make its 10 am from Euston a train for Edinburgh and Glasgow only, and to christen it the "Royal Scot". A second train would make the intermediate stops, and the only compulsory halt was that at Symington in Scotland, where the Edinburgh and Glasgow portions parted company. A new 15-coach train had been built, with nine coaches for Glasgow and six for Edinburgh and with restaurant cars in both portions, and new and more powerful locomotives were on order, though not ready in time for the opening of the non-stop operation on July 11 of that year.

In order to bring the locomotive working within reasonable limits for the engine-crews concerned,

it was decided that there should be an intermediate stop, at Carnforth in Lancashire, to change engines; between Euston and Carnforth, 236¼ miles, the motive power was an ex-London & North Western Claughton 4-6-0 piloted by a George the Fifth 4-4-0, while for the 165¼ miles over Shap and Beattock summits on to Glasgow a pair of the Midland compound 4-4-0s, with Scottish crews, were responsible. Not to be outdone, from the same date the London & North Eastern Railway began operating the "Flying Scotsman" non-stop over the 268¼ miles between Kings Cross and Newcastle with its Gresley Pacifics.

The LMSR working was in force during the summer of 1927 only, but before it ceased the first of the new Royal Scot 4-6-0s had made their appearance, and experiments had been made with non-stop running over the 301 miles between Euston and Kingmoor, Carlisle. Coming events thus cast their shadows before. So the announcement that from May 1 the "Royal Scot" would run daily without any intermediate stop between London and Carlisle caused no surprise. But the LNER was not to be caught napping. In conditions of the greatest secrecy at Doncaster Gresley had been building some unique corridor tenders which would provide a through passage between the "Flying Scotsman" train and the footplate of its Pacific locomotive, and so permit a relief crew daily to take over the working of the locomotive at the midway point in a world record non-stop run of 392¾ miles between Kings Cross and Edinburgh. Not only so, but the rival line was

▼ The "Corridor"—best-known of all West Coast trains in LNWR days, the 2 pm from Euston, with the set of 12-wheel stock introduced in 1908, headed by Claughton 4-6-0 No. 2097.

putting into service a brand new "Flying Scotsman" train with such amenities as a hairdressing saloon, a cocktail bar and a retiring room for ladies. May 1, 1928, was the opening date.

This was competition with a vengeance, for the LMSR could not arrange any regular non-stop run longer than the 365¾ miles between Euston and Symington, and in event was not likely to attempt anything more than the Euston-Carlisle run with a single engine-crew. But the LNER did not quite have the last word. With sly humour, and again in conditions of great secrecy, on the Friday before the new workings were to begin, the LMSR authorities divided the "Royal Scot" into two parts, and ran both without any stop between starting-point and destination. The 401½ miles achieved by Royal Scot 4-6-0 No. 6113

Cameronian with its nine-coach train between Euston and Glasgow was a British record for any type of locomotive up to that date, while compound No. 1054's 399¾ miles between Euston and Edinburgh was probably the longest non-stop run in railway history achieved by any 4-4-0 locomotive. So by these ingenious proceedings the LMSR certainly stole some of the LNER thunder!

In the following year, another Anglo-Scottish non-stop run of note was achieved by a Royal Scot 4-6-0, in this case No. 6127 *Novelty*. In connection with the opening of a new coal distillation plant at Glenboig, where the Caledonian main line from the south joins that from Buchanan Street to Aberdeen, a special train was run for the returning guests without a stop over the 395½ miles from Glenboig to Euston in 7 hr. 58 min. This

▲ The down "Royal Scot", with the 15-coach train set when newly named in 1927, headed by new Royal Scot 4-6-0 No. 6139 *Ajax*, passing Bushey on its non-stop run to Carlisle.   [F. R. Hebron

▼ When the LMSR stole the LNER thunder—Midland compound 4-4-0 No. 1054 on the 400-mile non-stop run from Euston to Edinburgh, three days before the inauguration of the East Coast non-stop London–Edinburgh run of the "Flying Scotsman".

was an even more notable feat than the previous Euston-Glasgow non-stop run, for not only was it faster, but as compared with *Cameronian*'s nine-coach train *Novelty* was hauling twelve coaches, including two cinema cars, a lounge and an observation saloon.

It is interesting to recall, however, that all these non-stop records were beaten by the rival "Flying Scotsman" in 1948, the first year of nationalisation, when disastrous floods had cut the East Coast main line between Berwick and Dunbar, and the East Coast trains had to be diverted temporarily by way of Galashiels and Kelso. On several occasions the up train ran the 408½ miles from Edinburgh to Kings Cross by this route without a stop—probably the longest non-stop runs with steam power not only in British but in world history.

The ludicrous feature of the non-stop West and East Coast runs that began in 1927 was that the dead hand of the 1896 agreement as to minimum times was still operating. Although all but two West Coast and the whole of the East Coast intermediate stops by the trains concerned had been excised, the public 8¼-hr. schedules still remained (with a few minutes less in the working timetables), and so continued for nearly four years, until 1932. At last, however, with train services in all other directions being speeded up,

this lethargy of the Anglo-Scottish trains could no longer be tolerated. The LMSR and LNER managements therefore agreed to abandon the 1896 agreement, but with this important proviso. They would keep each other advised of any improvements of their Anglo-Scottish services that they had in prospect, and particularly of any accelerations; there were to be no more secret preparations by one rival to take the other by surprise.

So, in the subsequent years, a considerable advance took place. It must be admitted that in most developments the LNER took the lead, with the LMSR following, but in many respects very little if at all behind. The "Royal Scot" had its time from Euston to Glasgow cut by 25 min., to 7 hr. 50 min., and when non-stop running was resumed in the summer timetable to 7 hr. 40 min. each way, an acceleration of 35 min. On the other side of the country the "Flying Scotsman", also speeded up to 7 hr. 50 min. between Kings Cross and Edinburgh in May, had no less than 45 min. cut from its non-stop schedule in the summer timetable. These changes had a tonic effect on

▼ Climbing Grayrigg Bank—Royal Scot 4-6-0 No. 6132 *Phoenix* passes Oxenholme with the down "Midday Scot". Next the engine is a through GWR coach from Plymouth to Glasgow.   [F. R. Hebron

▲ Attacking Shap—4-6-2 No. 46206 *Princess Marie Louise* passes Tebay with a Birmingham–Glasgow express. [J. E. Wilkinson]

speed all over the country, not only on the other services of the competing railways, but on other lines as well.

By 1936 competition once again was hotting up. In May 1932 the LMSR suddenly selected the one-time "Corridor", now the "Midday Scot", to such revolutionary treatment as to make it the fastest train of the day between Euston and Glasgow. Reverting from 1.30 to its former 2 pm departure from Euston, it was booked into Glasgow at 9.35 pm; 7 hr. 35 min. was 30 min. less than its previous time and 45 min. less that that operating before the accelerations of 1932. The schedule involved the Stanier Pacifics in working a train of from 445 to over 500 tare tons in weight over the 51.2 miles from Lancaster to Penrith—Shap summit included—in 59 min. start to stop, probably the most exacting locomotive task in Great Britain at that date.

The LNER reply was not long in coming. It came in July with an acceleration of the 1.20 pm from Kings Cross to reach Edinburgh at 8.45 pm, 20 min. earlier, in 7 hr. 25 min. from Kings Cross. The corresponding 2.5 pm from Edinburgh came down to a 7½-hr. run, reaching London at 9.35 pm. The non-stop "Flying Scotsman" by now was making the journey in 7¼ hr., and with a new connection from Edinburgh, Aberdeen was reached

in 10 hr. 28 min. from London—a 57 min. acceleration.

The next development recalled some of the excitements of the 1888 and 1895 Races. In 1935 the LNER had set a precedent of note by intro-ducing Britain's first streamlined train—the "Silver Jubilee"—running the 268¼ miles between Kings Cross and Newcastle in 4 hr., and requiring sustained speeds up to 90 mph for timekeeping. Speeds up to 113 mph had been reached with its streamlined A4 Pacifics, and the publicity that it had been earning was inducing some distinct restlessness on the LMSR side. So successful had the "Silver Jubilee" been financially that the LNER, looking round for fresh fields to conquer, decided to experiment with a similar streamliner between Kings Cross and Edinburgh, taking no more than 6 hr. for the journey of 392.7 miles. Moreover, as its introduction would take place in the same year as the Coronation of King George VI, what more suitable name for it than "Coronation"?

The LNER intentions were revealed to the LMSR management in the autumn of 1936, and the latter was compelled to consider seriously what must be done about such a competitive service. Actually the first thing the LMSR did was to stage an experimental non-stop run from Euston to Glasgow and back on November 16 and 17, 1936. With a seven-coach train of 225 tons tare and 230 tons gross Stanier Pacific No. 6201 *Princess Elizabeth* covered the 401.4 miles in the down direction in 5 hr. 53 min. 38 sec., and on the

following day, with eight coaches and in bad weather conditions, made the return run in 5 hr. 44 min. 15 sec., at the astonishing average speed of precisely 70 mph. This showed that even over the longer LMSR course a 6-hr. Euston-Glasgow timing might not be an impossibility.

But when July 1937 came, and with it the introduction of the LMSR "Coronation Scot" and the LNER "Coronation", the LMSR reply in many ways was a disappointment. Whereas Gresley of the LNER had built two of the finest sets of coaches ever seen in Great Britain for the "Coronation" workings, completely streamlined and including a beaver-tail observation car, the LMSR trains, though painted in distinctive blue-and-white colours, differed little internally from the company's standard stock. More disappointing still was the LMSR schedule. Notwithstanding the amazing performance of *Princess Elizabeth* in the previous November, and the LNER "Coronation's" 6-hr. timing, the LMSR had decided on nothing more exacting than 6½ hr., including a 2-min. stop at Carlisle.

One feature of the LMSR reply, however, was certainly not a disappointment. It was that Stanier, the Chief Mechanical Engineer, had been spurred on to design a completely streamlined Pacific for the workings. And on June 29, 1937, No. 6220 *Coronation*, the first of the class, was to show its paces. The LNER maximum speed record at that time stood at 113 mph, and though the fact was not disclosed to those travelling on the train on the occasion of the Press trip, there is no question that the LMSR authorities were determined, if they could, to achieve something higher. To do this the help of gravity was needed,

and the only possible location on the main line from Euston to Crewe was the 10½ miles down from the summit at Whitmore.

Down this grade Driver Clarke was encouraged to some reckless running which produced a top speed of 114 mph no more than a mile or slightly over from the series of cross-over roads leading into Crewe Station, the first of which, after violent braking, was struck at 57 instead of the prescribed 20 mph. The LMSR had thus secured its record, but at the price of a hairbreadth escape from disaster. Providentially, no damage had been done to the engine or to the train, and on the return that day No. 6220 *Coronation*, with an eight-coach load of 263 tons tare and 270 tons gross, achieved a time of 119 min. precisely over the 158 miles from Crewe to Euston—a time that would remain unbeaten until in the electric age of the nationalised British Railways it became the standard time for many up expresses over this course.

So Anglo-Scottish rivalry between the West and East Coast Routes reached its climax in the late 1930s. By 1939 war once again laid its heavy hand on all railway progress—indeed, a heavier hand than in 1914–1918. After its conclusion, in 1945, recovery from its devastating effects was painfully slow, and by the beginning of 1948 the London Midland & Scottish and London & North Eastern Railways as such, and the competition between them, had ceased to exist.

"AT DERBY the nice little engines were made pets of. They were housed in nice clean sheds and were very lightly loaded. There must have been a Royal Society for the Prevention of Cruelty to Engines in existence. At Horwich they had all gone scientific, and talked in 'thous', although apparently some of their work was to the nearest half-inch. At Crewe they just didn't care so long as their engines could roar and rattle along with a good paying load, which they usually did." Such was the amusing comment of D. W. Sanford in the discussion that followed the reading in 1946 by E. S. Cox to the Institution of Locomotive Engineers of a highly informative paper entitled "A Modern Locomotive History". This described in uninhibited fashion what had taken place on the LMSR in the locomotive realm during the first ten years from the formation of the group in 1923.

Sanford's commentary gave a not altogether inaccurate picture of LMSR locomotive conditions during this period. The Midland Railway had certainly specialised in small engines and light trains; for handling loads on the fastest passenger services limited to 260 tons maximum with their most powerful class, Derby had never built anything larger than 4-4-0s. Equally with freight the 0-6-0 wheel arrangement had been the limit, with the result that all the heavy coal trains between the Nottinghamshire coalfields and London had to be double-headed. The only more powerful engines that had emerged from Derby up till then were the eleven 2-8-0s built in 1914 for the 1 in 50 gradients of the Somerset & Dorset Joint Line and the one and only "Big Emma" 0-10-0 turned out five years later to help in banking duties on the

1 in 37¾ Lickey incline. Henry Fowler had been in charge of Midland locomotive policy from 1909 onwards.

Sanford's description of LNWR locomotive working also was not inapt. Following on the exploits of the Great Western 4-cylinder 4-6-0 *Polar Star* in the locomotive exchange of 1910, Bowen Cooke had designed and built at Crewe the 4-cylinder Claughtons, but without repeating the GWR success; otherwise many of the principal LNWR trains were still being handled by George the Fifth 4-4-0s and Prince of Wales 4-6-0s, which with substantial loads had to be worked very hard to keep time. In such conditions coal consumption was heavy. Freight was being handled mainly by 0-8-0 locomotives. At the end of 1920 Hewitt Beames had taken over at Crewe after the sudden death of Bowen Cooke, but the former's tenure of office as Chief Mechanical Engineer had lasted no more than a year. For in 1922, a year before the grouping, the London & North Western and Lancashire & Yorkshire Railways had amalgamated, and the latter's CME, George Hughes, being the senior, had taken over the office. The L&YR, with its severe gradients, had not been reluctant to invest in powerful locomotives, among them the Hughes 4-cylinder 4-6-0s and many powerful 0-8-0s, but like the "Claughtons" the former had not been outstandingly successful.

Of the other constituents of the LMSR the most important was the Caledonian Railway in Scotland. Here J. F. McIntosh had established a reputation with his various Dunalastair 4-4-0 classes and his handsome Cardean 4-6-0s, but his successor from 1914 onwards, William Pickersgill, had made no great mark. Still less so on the Glasgow & South Western had Peter Drummond, successor from 1912 to James Manson, during the six years to 1918, when Robert Harben Whitelegg

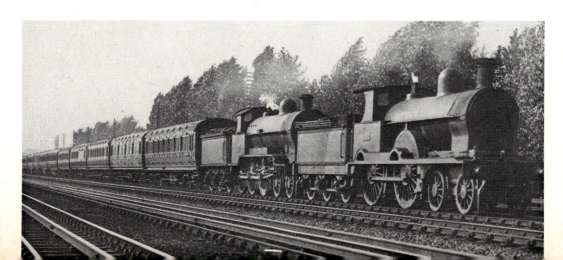

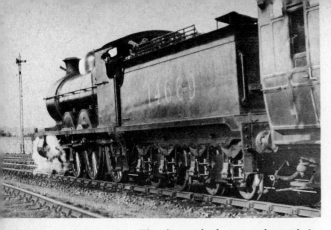

took over. The latter had not enhanced his reputation when Locomotive Superintendent of the London Tilbury & Southend Railway by building eight massive 4-6-4 tank engines for the Southend passenger service which the Great Eastern Railway refused to accept over the viaduct into Fenchurch Street terminus because of excessive weight; these became white elephants for which the Midland Railway, absorbing the LT&SR in 1912, could find no useful service. But Whitelegg was finding a better outlet for his designing talent on the G&SWR.

By a remarkable coincidence, another London Midland & Scottish constituent, the Highland Railway, had had as its Locomotive Superintendent from 1912 to 1915 an engineer who was relieved of his post after having designed and had built a series of 4-6-0 engines, the River class 4-6-0s, which the Civil Engineer, Alexander Newlands, absolutely refused to allow to run over the Highland main line. Unfortunately Smith had neglected to communicate any details of his new design to the Civil Engineer's Department, whose calculations showed the weight of the engines to be quite

inadmissible over a number of bridges, while their cross-sectional dimensions would have made for clearance difficulties also. This was a great pity, as the design was, for the period, technically superior to anything else in Scotland at that time. Eventually the Caledonian Railway took the engines over, but though they were considerably superior in performance to the Pickersgill "60" class 4-6-0s and still more so to the latter's sluggish 3-cylinder 4-6-0s, they were never given a chance to display their prowess—a fine design, indeed, thrown to waste.

Of the smaller LMSR constituents the most enterprising, from the locomotive point of view, had been the North Staffordshire Railway. Under J. H. Adams from 1902 to 1915 and J. A. Hookham from 1915 to 1922 an effective stud of locomotives had been built up, including some fine 4-4-2 and 0-6-4 tanks, and interesting experimental work had been done also, such as the building of a 4-cylinder 0-6-0 tank (later converted to a tender engine) with the cranks dividing the circle up into four parts—the first application of its kind in Great Britain. Other constituent companies contributed their quota of locomotive power—the Furness Railway, with some large 4-6-4 tanks; the Maryport & Carlisle; and the Wirral. The former North London Railway had been worked by the London & North Western Railway from 1908 onwards, but its unique 4-4-0 tank engines were still operating some of the suburban services out of Broad Street terminus.

So the London Midland & Scottish Railway began its 25-year history with a stock of 10,316 steam locomotives, of no fewer than 393 different types—a vast responsibility for its first Chief

▲ Manson 4-6-0 of the Glasgow & South Western Railway, numbered 14669 in the LMSR list, leaving Prestwick.   [M. W. Earley

▼ A typical Lancashire & Yorkshire 0-8-0 freight locomotive at work on the main line between Todmorden and Sowerby Bridge.

Mechanical Engineer. It would be difficult to say that amid this variety any class from any one of the constituent companies would go down to history as an outstanding type, either in the realm of tractive power or economical working, comparable, say, with a Churchward Star 4-6-0 on the Great Western Railway. Little had been done by any of the LMSR constituent companies to develop valve-setting of the kind which would permit short cut-off working with wide open regulators, associated with high working pressures. The traditional in these matters still held firm sway in the various locomotive works within the group. If any type could be regarded as breaking away from tradition, it was the 4-4-0 3-cylinder compounds of the Midland Railway which, in contra-distinction to the ineffectiveness of the many former Webb compounds on the London & North Western Railway, had shown that a well-designed compound could prove a capable and economical motive power unit.

Locomotive building on the newly-formed LMSR was concentrated mainly in five plants—the vast Crewe complex of the London & North Western Railway; Derby of the Midland; Horwich, formerly Lancashire & Yorkshire but now by the amalgamation of the previous year a second LNWR works; St. Rollox of the Caledonian; and Kilmarnock of the Glasgow & South Western. A certain amount of locomotive building had been carried out at the Stoke-on-Trent works of the North Staffordshire Railway, but this plant, like the Lochgorm (Inverness) works of the Highland Railway, the Barrow-in-Furness works of the Furness Railway, and the Plaistow works of the former London, Tilbury & Southend Railway,

had been concerned mainly with locomotive maintenance and repair.

In the appointments which were made to the principal LMSR locomotive positions, seniority proved to be the chief consideration. So, as previously mentioned, the task of Chief Mechanical Engineer fell to George Hughes, formerly CME of the Lancashire & Yorkshire, but promoted to the position of command at Crewe on the amalgamation of the two companies in the previous year. As his deputy he had Sir Henry Fowler, a former Horwich man who had been appointed Chief Mechanical Engineer to the Midland Railway in 1909, and who also was to remain in control at Derby as Mechanical Engineer, Midland Division. His opposite number as Mechanical Engineer, Crewe, continued to be Captain H. P. M. Beames, while the other Divisional Mechanical Engineers were G. N. Shawcross at Horwich, W. Pickersgill at St. Rollox, R. H. Whitelegg at Kilmarnock and J. A. Hookham at Stoke-on-Trent. All these men thus retained their previous charges, but now under the direction of the one LMSR Chief Mechanical Engineer.

▼ Climbing to Slochd Mhuic Summit, between Inverness and Aviemore—Highland Castle 4-6-0 No. 14684 (LMS numbering). [F. R. Hebron

▲ Most powerful LYR express passenger type—a Hughes 4-cylinder 4-6-0, LMSR No. 10420, taking water from Walkden troughs. [E. R. Wethersett

▲ Lancashire & Yorkshire superheated 2-4-2 tank No. 632. [LPC

▲ North Staffordshire 0-6-4 tank No. 119.　[BR　▼ Caledonian 4-6-2 tank No. 15359 (LMS numbering).

▲ Furness Railway 4-6-4 tank No. 11104 (LMS numbering). [F. R. Hebron

▲ London Tilbury & Southend 4-6-4 tank No. 2104 (Midland numbering) [LPC

▼ Glasgow & South Western Whitelegg 4-6-4 on 5.10 pm Glasgow to Ayr, with Pullman tea car. [M.W. Earley

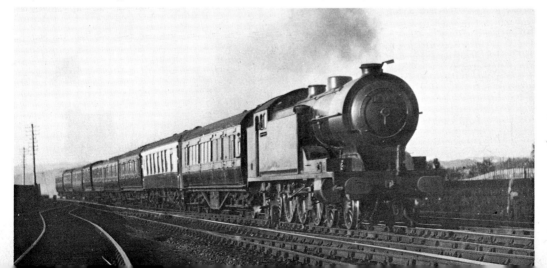

7 · *The Midland Influence, 1923–1931*

DURING THE settling down period that was inevitable after amalgamation on such a scale, there were few developments of note in the design realm. Horwich had had in preparation a massive 4-6-4 type tank, generally uniform with the Hughes 4-cylinder tender engines; ten of these entered service in 1924, but not to achieve the success anticipated. At Crewe Hewitt Beames had been responsible for a powerful 0-8-4 tank design, of which 29 were turned out in 1923 and one in 1924. Otherwise construction proceeded between 1923 and 1925 of various standard types of the different pre-grouping companies—Midland 4-4-0 compounds, 0-6-0 freight engines and 0-6-0 tanks; Lancashire & Yorkshire 4-6-0 express engines; London Tilbury & Southend 4-4-2 tanks; and one or two others.

Meantime, with the help of the up-to-date Horwich dynamometer car, tests were being conducted on an extensive scale to determine the average coal consumption and repair costs of the most numerous locomotive classes that were in use in the group. These had some remarkable results. Easily the most economical classes in terms of coal burned per mile were the Midland 4-4-0s, the Class 2 with 45.9 lb. and the Class 4 compound with 46.5 lb. The most extravagant 4-4-0s were the LNWR "George the Fifths", with 56.4 lb., the Pickersgill design of the Caledonian with 59.1 lb., and Peter Drummond's G&SW 4-4-0s with 63.4 lb. But even this figure was exceeded by Pickersgill's "60" class Caledonian 4-6-0s, which consumed an average of no less than 66.3 lb. of coal to the mile. By comparison, the LNWR Prince of Wales 4-6-0s made quite a good showing, with 51.1 lb. per mile only.

When it came to repair costs, however, the results were very different, save that the Midland Class 2 4-4-0, lowest in coal consumption, was cheapest in maintenance also. But now, remarkable to relate, the thermally inefficient but robustly-built Pickersgill Caledonian creations were near the top of the tree, the 4-4-0 averaging 110 and the "60" class 4-6-0 117, assuming the Midland Class 2 figure as 100. The LNWR George the Fifth 4-4-0 at 149 and the Prince of Wales 4-6-0 were both

36

inferior to the Midland compound 4-4-0 at 136. There is no doubt, therefore, that the last-mentioned design scored a triumph in these comparisons.

By reason of age, the tenure of office by George Hughes at the head of LMSR locomotive affairs was short, and in 1925 he was succeeded by Henry Fowler. This change made it pretty evident that for the time being Derby rather than Crewe would be the dominant influence in LMSR locomotive development. Now both men were convinced that larger and more powerful locomotives would be needed to cope with increasing demands of loads and speeds. During his reign at Horwich Hughes had completed the design of an enormous 4-cylinder 2-10-0 freight engine, with four 19 in. by 28 in. cylinders and a boiler built out to the extreme limits of the loading gauge, and the design was re-examined in 1924 as a possible means of doing away with the wasteful double-heading of Midland coal trains, but weak bridgework at various points on the Midland main line put the imposition of such a weight out of court. Before giving up his office, also, in 1924 Hughes had produced a Pacific design. Fowler, on his part, had prepared two notable designs, one for a 4-6-2 passenger engine and the other for a 2-8-2 freight engine, both to be 4-cylinder compounds with a working pressure of 240 lb. per sq. in.

But Fowler, unfortunately, was anything but a free agent. The controlling factor in all Midland Railway locomotive developments for long past had been the Motive Power Department, and from the formation of the LMSR these conditions remained unchanged. It would have been inconceivable on the Great Western Railway for such a man as Churchward to have been under the domination of any Superintendent of Operation, or on the LNER for Gresley to have been subject to any such limitation, but not so during the first ten years of the LMSR. And whatever Fowler might think, with the Midland J. E. Anderson firmly in the saddle as the LMSR Superintendent of Motive Power continuance of the Midland small engine policy, completely at variance with

Gresley's big engine policy on the LNER, was a foregone conclusion.

So it came about that in the five years from 1924 to 1928 no fewer than 530 Midland 0-6-0 freight engines, 371 Midland "Jinty" 0-6-0 tanks and 190 Midland 4-4-0 compounds were added to the LMSR stock. The compounds were distributed all over the system, and found their way on to the fast Euston-Birmingham trains, on which at first the "Crimson Ramblers", as they became known, were anything but popular. To drivers brought up in the London & North Western tradition, of working with long cut-offs, partly closed regulators and a fierce blast, attempts to work the compounds in the same way had unhappy results, and it took time before some of the drivers, like the redoubtable Laurie Earl, had mastered the proper handling of the unique Deeley regulator. In Scotland, however, it was not long before the compounds won their way into the hearts of the locomotivemen, who eventually were getting better work out of them than the Midland drivers themselves.

One type of engine badly needed on the LMSR during this period was a mixed traffic type, capable of reasonably fast passenger work when necessary, and in 1926 Horwich produced what was required. It was a 2-6-0 of unusual appearance, with outside cylinders perched high up for clearance reasons and inclined at a steep angle alongside the smoke-

box, and a high running-plate, completely exposing the cylinders, back to the cab. For the first time the LMSR now possessed a class of locomotive with long-travel long-lap valves, and the success of the "Crabs", as they soon became known, was immediate. They therefore became a standard class, a distinction shared up to the end of 1926 by three other classes only, all Midland—the 4-4-0 compounds, and the tender and tank 0-6-0s.

Not until 1926 did it dawn upon the LMSR administration that more powerful locomotives were needed to handle the principal passenger services. The operating authorities had certain Anglo-Scottish developments in prospect, but no locomotives capable of the performance which would be required without pilot assistance. In the previous year Sir Josiah Stamp had been appointed to the new post of President of the Executive, and though while he was gathering up the reins there had been no immediate effect on the locomotive side, there is little doubt that already he was making his presence felt. Anyway, there suddenly appeared on London Midland & Scottish metals the Great Western 4-cylinder 4-6-0 No.

5000 *Launceston Castle*, for some trial running between Euston and Carlisle. Precisely how this loan was arranged has always been wrapped in mystery; it was almost certainly over Fowler's head and probably was not unconnected with the triumph of the "Castles" over the Gresley Pacifics in the GWR-LNER exchange of the previous year.

The result of this new exchange was almost a foregone conclusion. Every task committed to *Launceston Castle* was mastered with consummate ease; I myself have vivid memories of a run southwards from Carlisle with the 10 am from Glasgow to Euston on which the GWR 4-6-0 with a 415-ton train had gained 13¼ min. on schedule by Preston alone, and achieved a net time of 157 min. to Crewe, or 19 min. less than that scheduled. From Rugby to Euston, 82.6 miles, in 86¼ min., or 82¼ min. net, with a gross load of 505 tons, was another notable feat; at the time I wrote "I should very much doubt if such a time as 15 min. 10 sec. from Bletchley up to Tring has ever been equalled in North Western annals, with such a load as this, or considerably less, and no pilot." Still more significant was the fact that

▲ 0-10-0 No. 2290, specially built for banking north-bound trains up the 1 in 37¾ of the Lickey incline (No. 58100 in the LMSR list). [P. B. Whitehouse

◀ Many Midland Class 2 4-4-0s were built under LMSR auspices. Here No. 655 is piloting a Royal Scot 4-6-0 on the up "Irish Mail", just after leaving Bangor. [Eric Treacy

▼ One of the numerous "Jinty" 0-6-0 tanks, used for a wide range of duties. This one is fitted with condensing gear for working through the Metropolitan tunnels. [LPC

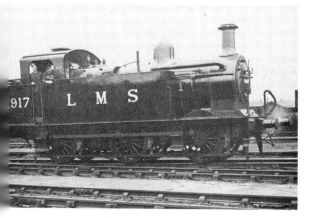

during these trials every previous record of locomotive efficiency made in the LMSR dynamometer car, in terms of power output relatively to coal consumption, had been soundly beaten by this most competent stranger.

The effect on higher LMSR circles was immediate and revolutionary, and seldom was the Chief Mechanical Engineer of a large and important railway overridden with such complete disregard to his authority as that to which Fowler was now subjected. Already, though the idea of such large engines was anathema to the Motive Power Department, he had laid down at Derby the first frames for his proposed compound Pacifics, and work on these he was now bidden peremptorily to stop. More humiliating still, he was instructed to obtain from Swindon Works a set of working drawings of the Castle 4-6-0; not surprisingly, however, as the Great Western was never forthcoming in locomotive matters, the request was refused. Maunsell of the Southern Railway, however, was more accommodating, and the working drawings of his new Lord Nelson 4-6-0s did find their way to Derby.

The matter was now urgent, for no more than ten months remained before the new LMSR showpiece Anglo-Scottish train, the "Royal Scot", was due to begin service. So at the end of 1926 a contract was placed with the North British Locomotive Company for fifty 4-6-0 engines, to be designed by the builders' own staff but under the supervision of Herbert Chambers, Chief Draughtsman at Derby, and incorporating such details of the SR Lord Nelson design as might be thought suitable. No more than eight months later, in August 1927, the first Royal Scot 4-6-0 had been delivered. To what extent the design had borrowed from the Maunsell engine has always been debatable; there was certainly little external resemblance, but in later years the extent to which the internals had derived from Southern practice was the subject of some lively interchanges between E. S. Cox of the LMSR and H. Holcroft of the SR. Anyway, the Royal Scots benefited by most of the best of then current locomotive practice, and at first were very successful; but after some years of service certain defects in the design began to manifest themselves, and seriously to increase their coal consumption. By and large, little of this design can be credited to Sir Henry Fowler; not until their rebuilding by his successor were these engines really to come into their own.

It was in the same year, 1927, that the question of the double-heading of Midland coal trains once again came under review. When it had become clear to Hughes that weight would prevent his big 2-10-0 from solving the problem, his thoughts had turned to the possibility of Beyer-Garratt articulation to spread the load. At last it was decided to make the experiment, and three 2-6-6-2 locomotives were ordered from the firm of Beyer Peacock. Although the makers were allowed freedom in their boilers and their chassis design, the cylinders and motion had to be "Midlandised", with no use of such current developments as long-travel long-lap valve-motions and other features that had been incorporated in the new Royal Scots. Although 30 more of these Garratts were bought in 1930, because of this shortsightedness they never achieved the complete success that they might have done, though they did bring much of the double-heading to an end.

In 1930 there was another significant happening. A number of experiments had been carried out to try to improve the performance of the LNWR Claughton 4-6-0s, and in this year, with experience that had been gained from the Royal Scots, two Claughtons were completely rebuilt on Royal Scot lines. The results were so successful that two years later a whole series of similar locomotives came into service, nominally rebuilds but actually to all intents and purposes new engines. Being a little lighter than the Royal Scots, the "Baby Scots", as they soon became known (though officially the Patriot class) could be used over certain routes from which the former for weight

▼ One of the Horwich-built 2-6-0 "Crabs", No. 42737 (BR numbering) passing Greskine box on the climb to Beattock Summit.   [W. S. Sellar

▲ Brand new out of Crewe works—Royal Scot 4-6-0 No. 6126. [BR

▼ Developed from the rebuilding of an LNWR Claughton 4-6-0—Patriot 4-6-0 No. 5527 *Southport* hard at work. [Eric Treacy

reasons were excluded, in particular the North Staffordshire main line through Stoke-on-Trent. Their toughest task was the 12.10 pm Lancastrian from Manchester to Euston, on which I often recorded their performance, and found them most speedy and capable engines.

Other developments of this period were the introduction in 1927 of a new standard 2-6-4 tank type, and two years later of a new standard 0-8-0 class; of the former, up to 1932, 85 were turned out, and of the latter, to the same date, 175. The Horwich 2-6-0s were multiplied to a total of 245 between 1926 and 1932, and between 1928 and 1932 138 Midland Class 2 4-4-0s took the rails—the latter a rather poor addition to an already under-powered stock. Including 70 Royal Scots, in the ten years up to 1932 the LMSR locomotive stud had been increased by 2,002 units, almost entirely of Midland types, and by a modest 156 of non-standard types.

And why the emphasis on 1932? Because this was the year in which a radical change was brought about in the locomotive administration of the London Midland & Scottish Railway. Sir Josiah Stamp had been in office from 1926 as President of the Executive, and had become increasingly restive at the state of affairs in the company's Locomotive Department. There was still no love lost between Derby and Crewe, and with each works maintaining its former traditions there was little co-operation either. In Scotland the Caledonian authorities, proud of their sturdy

and trouble-free locomotives (even if their coal-eating propensities were on the extravagant side!) strove to maintain their resistance to Midland interference.

While the Midland building policy certainly had achieved a great deal in the direction of standardisation, the railway as a whole still had far too many locomotives and too many classes, and yet at the same time inadequate power, and there was little chance of any material improvement unless something drastic was done. In fact, to control the warring elements it needed a strong man to be brought in from outside, and this is precisely what the LMSR Executive did. At the beginning of 1931 Fowler was quietly shunted to the position of Assistant to the Vice-President for Works; for a year the CME seat was kept warm by E. J. H. Lemon, who up till then had been Carriage and Wagon Superintendent; and then, on January 1, 1932, the strong man whom the Executive had in view took office. He was W. A. Stanier, who for forty years had served the Great Western Railway at Swindon Works, and finally as Principal Assistant to the GWR Chief Mechanical Engineer. Such was one of the most sensational appointments in British railway history, and one which was to bestow immeasurable benefits on the London Midland & Scottish Railway.

▼ An experiment with turbo-condensing—the odd-looking Beyer Peacock Ljungström design during experimental running in 1926 over the Midland main line.   [BR

8 · Stanier takes Command

So JANUARY 1, 1932, saw the beginning of a revolution in London Midland & Scottish locomotive affairs, and of a phase in the life story of its central figure that was to mark him out as one of the most distinguished locomotive engineers in British railway history. The commission which Stanier had received from Stamp was clear-cut. It was drastically to reduce the LMSR locomotive stock, replacing its weaker and more inefficient elements by locomotives embodying all the latest developments, which would help towards economy in coal consumption and maintenance costs, and so lead to greater availability and greater mileages per engine. Already a great deal had been done to speed up and improve the maintenance work at both Crewe and Derby; similar improvements were now needed to the locomotives themselves. And in this matter Stanier was to have a free hand; no longer would the operating authorities be able to control what was being done in the design realm.

In selecting his principal lieutenants Stanier acted with considerable diplomacy. So far as concerned England his favours were distributed fairly equally between Crewe and Derby. At Crewe it had been a disappointment to Hewitt Beames that after acting for a year as LNWR Chief Mechanical Engineer he had to take second place to George Hughes on the LNWR–LYR amalgamation in 1922; and now in 1932 once again he had to play second fiddle, as Deputy Chief Mechanical Engineer, and this time to the stranger from Swindon. The Chief Draughtsman was still H. Chambers of Derby, while S. J. Symes of Derby was appointed Personal Assistant to the new CME, but these men did not necessarily share the "small engine" fixation of J. E. Anderson, who was still Superintendent of Motive Power. Not for long, however, as at the end of 1932 he retired. The road ahead was now clear for the momentous developments about to take place.

The first sign of Swindon influence was not long in coming. It was an externally transformed 2-6-0 with domeless taper boiler and other characteristic Swindon details. This was but a curtain-raiser, however, to what all locomotive enthusiasts were eagerly awaiting, when at midsummer, 1933, there rolled out of Crewe Works the biggest and most powerful express engine that had been built there up to that date—4-6-2 No. 6200, soon to be named *The Princess Royal*.

Many of the dimensions and details, such as the four 16¼ in. by 28 in. cylinders, the 6 ft. 6 in. coupled wheels, the 250 lb. pressure, and the high firebox sloping backwards and inwards to the cab, closely resembled those of the Great Western Kings, but Stanier had avoided the temptation to concentrate his power on the relatively short 4-6-0 King wheelbase (more or less compelled by the curvature of the West of England main line). On the other hand he had paid no attention to the previous aversion of the LMSR Motive Power Department to the use of more than three cylinders. So No. 6200, like a King, was a four-cylinder machine, and with the same tractive effort, 40,300 lb.

For three years, while experience was being gained with the new Pacifics, two only of the class were in service, Nos. 6200 and 6201. The latter, *Princess Elizabeth*, won distinction for herself in November 1934, with the non-stop runs over the 401½ miles from Euston to Glasgow and back described in Chapter 5, when in the up direction a time of 5 hr. 44¼ min. entailed an end-to-end average of 70 mph. By and large, however, the two Pacifics at first were not the outstanding success anticipated because Stanier had carried his Swindon principles too far. His former Chief, Churchward, had always proclaimed that he saw no purpose in throwing high temperature superheat out of the chimney; it was only necessary to "dry" the steam sufficiently to prevent condensation as it expanded in the cylinders. So at first the Pacific superheaters had 16 elements only.

Now while this principle had worked well with Welsh coal and GWR methods of firing, it was a different matter with the hard coals and the firing methods to which LMSR engine-crews were accustomed, with their long cut-offs and the sharpened exhausts of their engines. So it was that the boilers of all Stanier's earliest designs, the Pacifics included, after a short time had to be modified, at considerable expense to the Company, by considerable increases in the number of their superheater elements. With the Pacifics, for example, the superheating surface had to be increased from 370 to 653 sq. ft., now with 32 elements, and certain improvements to the draughting also had to be carried out. The performance of the engines from then on was greatly improved, as was demonstrated by *The

▲ An unhappy high pressure experiment—the Fowler super-pressure compound 4-6-0 No. 6399 *Fury*, carrying steam at 900 lb/sq in., which never entered revenue service.   [BR

▼ LMSR No. 6170 *British Legion* incorporating the chassis and other parts of *Fury*, which formed the prototype of the Royal Scot rebuildings.   [W. Potter

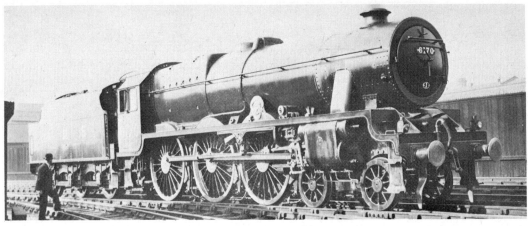

▼ Rebuilt Royal Scot No. 6170 *British Legion*, in its final form, leaving Preston with an express for the north.
                    [Eric Treacy

▶ One of the first two Stanier Pacifics—No. 46201 *Princess Elizabeth*, which greatly distinguished herself in November 1936 by working an 8-coach train from Glasgow to Euston, $401\frac{1}{2}$ miles, in 5 hr. $44\frac{1}{4}$ min. She is seen here passing Clifton with a Glasgow–Birmingham train.   [Eric Treacy

Princess Royal working a 15-coach train of 475 gross tons from Crewe to Willesden Junction, 152.7 miles, in 129 min. 33 sec., at a start-to-stop average of 70.7 mph. The way was now cleared for the turning out in 1935 of the next ten of the class, Nos. 6203 to 6212 inclusive.

But what of the missing number, 6202? This was the subject of a remarkable experiment—propulsion by a steam turbine instead of by conventional cylinders and motion. The boiler of No. 6202 was generally uniform with that of Nos. 6200 and 6210; but the turbine propulsion, comprising the main forward turbine and a smaller turbine for working in reverse, was based on the successful Ljungström experiments that had been taking place in Sweden. The main purpose of Stanier's test was to see if the cost of maintaining cylinders and motion could be reduced by the far more even torque of turbine propulsion. In normal service No. 6202 equalled the performance of Nos. 6200 and 6201, and at maximum output was definitely superior, but there were so many turbine failures of different kinds that after World War II it was decided to rebuild the engine as a normal Pacific. So, in the autumn of 1952, she re-emerged from Crewe Works as No. 6202 *Princess Anne*, but, alas, for a very short life only, as on October 8 of that year she was completely wrecked in the disastrous double collision at Wealdstone.

From 1933 onwards new construction at Crewe and Derby, as well as by outside builders, pro-ceeded rapidly. One of the most urgent needs was for a mixed traffic type of considerably greater power and speed capacity than the Hughes 2-6-0s, and here Stanier scored one of his most notable successes. It was his famous "Black Five", a 4-6-0 in Power Class 5 with 6-ft. coupled wheels and 18½ in. by 28 in. cylinders, which with its modest weight of 72 tons and limited cross-sectional dimensions would be able to go almost anywhere on the LMSR system. It was ten years earlier that Churchward at Swindon had taken a 6 ft. 8 in. 4-6-0, *Saint Martin*, and rebuilt it with 6-ft. wheels as the first of 329 Hall class mixed traffic engines; the new Stanier 6 ft. LMSR 4-6-0 had many similarities to the GWR engines. Eventually it became the most ubiquitous class on the LMSR system, built to a total of no fewer than 842 units, which were equally at home on fast passenger work up to 90 mph, express freight, and mountain climbing such as that on the Highland line. Their construction continued well into the years after nationalisation. The "Black Five" was one of the outstanding designs for which Stanier will be best remembered.

In the same year, 1934, a 3-cylinder 4-6-0 appeared which was designed to be roughly equal in power to the 3-cylinder Patriot 4-6-0s. The first example was No. 5552 *Silver Jubilee*. This was one of the classes with which Stanier made his initial error of low temperature superheat only, and of which the steaming of the earliest examples was poor; but a change to high superheat and

▲ An experiment in turbine propulsion—Stanier's
Pacific No. 6202, at speed with a Liverpool–Euston
express.   [Eric Treacy

▼ Stanier's masterpiece—one of his Duchess Pacifics in
BR days, No. 46223 *Princess Alice*, climbing Beattock
Bank with a London–Glasgow sleeping car express.
                                            [Eric Treacy

improved draughting cured the troubles, after which the Jubilees did excellent work. In particular they became for a number of years the mainstay of the express passenger services over the Midland main line, and were much used also between Euston, Birmingham and Wolverhampton.

New designs now followed one another rapidly. An end of the long reign of 4-4-2 tanks on the London Tilbury & Southend line was foreshadowed by a new series of 2-6-4 tanks, a development of the Fowler 2-6-4s but with three instead of two cylinders, for the exacting Fenchurch Street-Southend duties. Not surprisingly, in view of the success of the Churchward 4 ft. 8 in. freight 2-8-0s on the Great Western Railway, it was on the 2-8-0 wheel arrangement, rather than on the 0-8-0 so widely in use on the LMSR to that date, that Stanier decided for heavy freight haulage. The first Stanier 2-8-0, No. 8000, entered service in 1935, and eventually was built to a total of 719 engines. Much of this construction took place during World War II, and in addition to Crewe and outside builders, was distributed between the works of the other three groups at Swindon, Doncaster, Darlington, Eastleigh, Ashford and Brighton. A number of the engines went to railways in the Middle East to help the war effort. Another new LMSR arrival during 1935 was a small 2-6-2 tank type for suburban service. All these classes, needless to say, incorporated taper boilers and outside cylinders, and bore a general family likeness.

A further development in 1935 was of considerable importance. Six years earlier general interest had been aroused in certain European countries in the possibility of using compound propulsion in association with much higher pressures than ever previously considered with steam locomotion. Following this trend, in 1929 Gresley of the LNER evolved his 4-6-4 No. 10000 with a marine water-tube boiler pressed to 450 lb./sq. in.; while in the following year Sir Henry Fowler produced his No. 6399 *Fury*, a 4-6-0 in certain respects uniform with the Royal Scots but equipped with a Schmidt-type super-pressure boiler, part of which was designed to work at a pressure of no less than 900 lb./sq. in.

Unhappily, during an experimental run soon after construction, *Fury* lived up to its name by bursting a high pressure steam-pipe, the resulting outrush of steam killing a technician who was riding on the footplate. The engine was never steamed again, but certain parts, including the main frames, were still on hand when Stanier

decided on some experiments to improve the performance of the Royal Scots. These parts were therefore used in what, for accounting purposes, was described as a "rebuilding", though the end product, 4-6-0 No. 6170 *British Legion*, was to all intents and purposes a new engine.

There were a few teething troubles, but when these had been overcome a programme was initiated for "rebuilding" the whole of the Royal Scot class on similar lines. Again the products were to a large extent new engines, and once again Stanier had scored a bull's-eye. The converted "Scots" had no superiors if, indeed, any equals in performance among British 4-6-0s, and this was proved up to the hilt by their outstanding exploits during the exchange of locomotives from the different groups that immediately followed nationalisation in 1948, when their performances equalled those of some of their Pacific competitors.

We now come to 1936, when the LMSR had been advised of the LNER intention to introduce the streamlined 6-hr. "Coronation" between London and Edinburgh in the following year, and so had to do something serious to meet the new competition. As yet no more than the original 12 Pacifics of the Princess Royal type had entered service, and some new 4-6-2s, specially designed with sustained high speed in view, were needed. Such was the challenge that produced No. 6220 *Coronation*, Stanier's first streamlined Pacific, in 1937. Apart from an increase in driving wheel

▼ One of the Stanier Jubilee type 4-6-0s, No. 5630 *Swaziland*, on intermediate express passenger duty.

diameter from 6 ft. 6 in. to 6 ft. 9 in., the dimensions in general were the same as those of the previous Pacifics, but various refinements were incorporated to improve the performance. The speed capacity of the new engines was amply demonstrated on the trial trip on June 29, 1937 (described in Chapter 5) of the new "Coronation Scot" train, when a top speed of 114 mph was reached.

As to maximum power output, one of the most notable performances in British locomotive history was that of No. 6234 *Duchess of Abercorn* on February 26, 1939, with a 20-coach train of 610 tons from Crewe to Glasgow and back. Southbound, the train was worked over the 102.3 miles from Glasgow to Carlisle in 106 min. 30 sec., 9½ min. inside the schedule that had been laid down, and only 1½ min. more than the daily schedule of the 297-ton "Coronation Scot". Drawbar horsepowers of 1,800 to 2,000 were maintained over considerable distances, and on the final 1 in 99 from the north up to Beattock Summit, completed at 62 mph on this run, a drawbar hp. up to 2,511 was recorded, which meant an indicated hp. of at least 3,330.

By the outbreak of war in 1939, 20 of the class had entered service, 15 streamlined and 5 non-streamlined. Because of the wartime demand for maximum passenger power, building continued during the war, at first of streamlined and later of non-streamlined engines, the final example, No. 6257 *City of Salford*, being actually turned out in the first year of nationalisation, 1948. Its immediate predecessor, No. 6256, received the distinction of being named after its designer *Sir William A. Stanier, FRS*, whose eminent services to locomotive engineering had been rewarded by a knighthood in 1943. Eventually all 24 streamlined Pacifics had their streamlined casings removed, and until re-boilered could

▲ Most ubiquitous of all Stanier designs, his highly successful Class 5 mixed traffic 4-6-0. No. 45084 is here seen climbing the 1 in 60 to Glen Ogle, on the Callander & Oban line.   [W. J. V. Anderson

always be distinguished from the remainder by the rather ugly downward slope of the smokebox ahead of the chimney. In all, adding the 38 Coronation 4-6-2s to the 12 of the Princess series (but excluding the ill-fated *Princess Anne*), the total number of LMSR Pacifics reached 50, and represented one of the finest steam locomotive developments in British history.

But Stanier's mind had travelled a good deal further than this. As early as 1938 drawings had been prepared for a locomotive which would have put anything else in the country completely in the shade. It would have been a streamlined 4-6-4, with four 17½ in. by 28 in. cylinders, 6 ft. 6 in. coupled wheels, a boiler tapering to a maximum diameter of 6 ft. 10½ in., 70 sq. ft. of firegrate

▼ Another Stanier success was his standard 2-8-0 for heavy freight service, of which No. 8080 is a typical example.

The Stanier 2-6-4 tanks were a development of the Fowler design. No. 42571 pilots Jubilee 4-6-0 No. 45555 *Quebec* (BR numbering) up Shap incline with a Birmingham–Glasgow express.   [Derek Cross]

(mechanically fired), 300 lb. pressure, a tractive effort of 42,850 lb., and a weight in working order of 119 tons. With an 8-wheel tender accommodating 5,000 gal. of water and 12 tons of coal, engine and tender would have weighed 187 tons. Stanier's aim was to produce a locomotive which would have been capable of observing the "Coronation Scot" timings between Euston and Glasgow with a load up to 600 tons. But the outbreak of war put paid to this ambitious plan.

With the heavy hand of war again on the country, development in the locomotive realm was at a standstill during the remainder of Stanier's term of office, which came to an end early in 1944. By then, in addition to many other distinctions, he had had the unique honour among locomotive

▼ Built for service in Northern Ireland—5 ft. 3 in. gauge 2-6-0 No. 90 of the Northern Counties Committee.

engineers, shared only by Robert Stephenson many years before, of being elected a Fellow of the Royal Society. The CME chair was then kept warm temporarily by C. E. Fairburn, but with most of the work carried out by his able lieutenants, as he was an electrical rather than a steam expert. His period of office was very short, however, as in the following year he died, at the relatively early age of 58. The only original product of his brief reign, and one usually coupled with his name, was a modified type of 2-6-4 tank. Next in succession was H. G. Ivatt, who bore a family name honoured in locomotive engineering from the days of his father, H. A. Ivatt, of the Great Northern Railway. With nationalisation now looming ahead, no new designs were envisaged.

But with the inauguration of British Railways in 1948, London Midland & Scottish Railway locomotive history had not come to an end—far from it. For in 1946 R. A. Riddles, who from 1935 had been Stanier's Principal Assistant, joined the LMSR Board as Vice-President in charge of all engineering matters, and this led, in 1948, to his becoming the member of the Railway Executive responsible for mechanical and electrical engineering. With two lieutenants from Stanier's former staff, R. C. Bond as his Chief Officer for Locomotive Construction and Maintenance and E. S. Cox as his Executive Officer for Design, continuance of the Stanier tradition was assured, and a number of the earliest British Railways standard types were but slightly modified versions of the LMSR classes introduced during Stanier's reign. In no more than twelve years, therefore, from 1932 to 1944, Stanier had an influence on British locomotive design that was probably greater than that of any other engineer, apart, perhaps, from his former Swindon chief, Churchward.

9 · Electrification and Dieselisation

LIVERPOOL was the first city in what later became London Midland & Scottish territory to witness a conversion from steam to electric traction. The year was 1903, and the remarkable fact was that the railway concerned, of great importance to communication between Liverpool and Birkenhead, with the whole of the Wirral and beyond, remained independent at the time of the grouping and right up to nationalisation. Its modest 4¾ route miles began in tunnel under Liverpool Central Station, continued in tunnel under the Mersey to Hamilton Square, Birkenhead, and there forked, the left-hand branch to Rock Ferry, where connection was made with the joint London & North Western and Great Western line to Chester, and the right-hand branch to Birkenhead Park, end-on junction with the Wirral Railway.

The importance of the Mersey Railway to this chapter, however, is that precisely fifty years after the opening of the Mersey-Wirral exchange station at Birkenhead Park, during the whole of which through passengers had to change, completion in 1938 by the LMSR of the Wirral electrification made possible the introduction of through electric trains between Liverpool Central and West Kirby. Long before this, however, there had been another important electric development in the area. One year after the electrification of the Mersey line, the Lancashire & Yorkshire Railway inaugurated electric working on its important commuter line between Liverpool Exchange, Seaforth and Southport.

The next electrification of an LMSR constituent was a curious one, and there is little information as to what prompted it. Up till 1908, when it took place, all British electrification had been with direct current and third-rail conduction, with the Liverpool lines at 650V dc. But the Midland Railway electrification of 1908, between Lancaster, Morecambe and Heysham, was with alternating current, at 6,600V, and, of course, with overhead conductors. What the Midland management had in view with this experimental installation had never been revealed; certainly the MR never followed it up on any other part of its system.

But in the following year the London Brighton & South Coast adopted the same system in the first of its London suburban electrifications, and continued extensively with overhead ac up to World War I. It is interesting to speculate on how British railway electrification might have developed after these MR and LBSCR overhead ac beginnings had not the LBSCR been enclosed between the South Eastern & Chatham and London & South Western third rail dc installations after the formation of the Southern Railway in 1923, which compelled the LBSCR conversion to third rail dc also.

In the London suburban area of the London &

▼ First electrification by an LMSR constituent company was that of the Lancashire & Yorkshire Railway between Liverpool and Southport, inaugurated in 1904. One of the original trains.

North Western Railway the decision to electrify at last was reached just before World War I. But it was not merely electrification that was involved. For throughout from Chalk Farm to Watford Junction an entirely new double-track line was built to carry the electric trains. At Chalk Farm an amazing new complex of lines, mostly in tunnel, was laid out in all directions to cut out all crossing by trains over one another's paths; then the new electric lines were carried through a new Primrose Hill Tunnel to Queens Park and Kensal Green, beyond which they diverged into a new and separate Willesden Junction station. From here they proceeded well away from the existing lines, with sidings in

between, until they swung round to burrow under the main line and reach Wembley Central. From here they paralleled the existing lines until from Bushey they swung away westwards from the main line to curve round and join the Rickmansworth branch and so reach the High Street Station in the heart of Watford, before curving back to join the main line at Watford Junction.

The new lines, at first steam operated, were brought into use throughout in 1913, and two years later the Bakerloo tube line had come up to the surface at Queens Park and linked up with these LNWR electric lines. For this reason the London Underground fourth-rail system of dc electrification had to be adopted throughout, so

▲ The Midland was the first British railway to experiment with overhead electrification at 6,600 V ac. A Lancaster–Morecambe train strengthened with ordinary stock for summer working.   [W. S. Garth

▼ The turn of London came in 1914 with the London & North Western suburban electrification, fourth-rail at 630 V dc. One of the original Oerlikon trains leaving Euston for Watford.   [G. M. Kichenside

that the tube trains might be able to work through to Watford. Now that the Bakerloo tube trains all stop short at Queens Park, however, there has been a change to third-rail dc at 630 volts. The London electrification was completed by the conversion of the line from Broad Street to Willesden Junction High Level and from there to South Acton, from which point the LNWR electric trains continued over London & South Western electric lines to Richmond.

During this period the Lancashire & Yorkshire Railway had also been busy on its second and third electrifications, this time in the Manchester area. The former Locomotive Superintendent, J. A. F. Aspinall, was now General Manager, and was keenly interested in the uses of electricity; hence the two electrifications which aroused a good deal of interest at the time. One was of the short branch from Bury to Holcombe Brook, electrified on the overhead system at 3,500V dc and brought into use in 1913; the contractors, Dick Kerr & Co, who wanted experience, equipped the line at their own cost, and operated it, but the experiment did not last long. A permanent conversion, however, was that of the line from Manchester Victoria to Bury, running through an increasingly popular residential district; dc was decided on, but at the unusually high voltage of 1,200, which made necessary some special wooden protection for the positive conductor rail, to prevent any accidental contact by the staff.

No more electrification of LMSR constituents

now took place up to the formation of the London Midland & Scottish Railway. The London & North Western and Great Central Railways had been joint owners of the Manchester South Junction & Altrincham Railway, a busy commuter line to the south of the city, and after this had passed with the grouping to the LMSR and LNER jointly, the two companies decided in the late 1920s on electrification. By now the Weir Commission, appointed to lay down a future national policy on railway electrification, had issued its report, and had recommended overhead conduction at 1,500V dc, which already had been tried successfully by the North Eastern Railway on its mineral line from Shildon to Middlesbrough.

So this was the system adopted on the MSJAR, and later decided on for the very much more important LNER electrification between Sheffield and Manchester. The latter, however, badly delayed by the 1939–1945 war and the necessity to bore a new Woodhead Tunnel, was not completed until after nationalisation, when the section between Dunford, at the east end of Woodhead Tunnel, and Manchester passed to the control of the London Midland Region. Then, in the last LMSR years, there came the final electrification carried out by the company, which was, as already

▼ The Manchester–Bury experimental Lancashire & Yorkshire electrification at the unusually high third-rail pressure of 1,200 V dc. Note the wooden protection to the conductor rail. [W. Hubert Foster

Electrification at 1,500 V dc overhead jointly by the LMSR and LNER in 1931 of the Manchester South Junction & Altrincham line. A train leaves Altrincham depot. [W. Hubert Foster

The last LMSR electrification, completed in 1938, of the former Wirral Railway system from Birkenhead, third rail at 650 V dc. [BR

mentioned, of the Wirral lines radiating from Birkenhead, third-rail at 650V dc, completed in 1938. Many years were to elapse before the 25,000V ac electrification which has transformed the London Midland main line service out of Euston became accomplished fact.

Coming events cast their shadows before. Another form of motive power now was destined to join with electricity in ousting steam from British rails, and that was the diesel engine. As far back as 1928, one of the Manchester-Bury four-coach electric sets was converted to diesel-electric propulsion, and put to work on a local shuttle service between Blackpool Central and Lytham. In the early 1930s some experiments were conducted with diesel-electric shunting; one remarkable conversion was the use of the chassis of a "Jinty" 0-6-0 steam shunting tank to mount on it a diesel engine with a mechanical transmission, which made its appearance as a rebuild in 1933. Similar experiments followed up to 1936,

by which time it had been realised that the continuous availability of a diesel-electric shunter gave it a considerable economical advantage over its steam counterpart, and so the reign of diesel shunting had begun. A further experiment with a diesel-propelled passenger train was made in 1938, when a handsome streamlined three-coach articulated set of 750 hp took the rails. After running-in between St. Pancras and Bedford it was used to provide a fast cross-country service between Oxford and Cambridge. But nothing seems to have come of this particular experiment.

Finally, in the very last year of independent LMSR history, there came one of the most important motive power developments of all. By the 1940s diesel traction was rapidly displacing steam on the main lines of the United States, and

▼ The LMSR pioneered with diesel shunting. Diesel-electric 350 hp. 0-6-0 No. 12026 at Carlisle.
[D. J. Sutton

the economic advantages were such as to make it clear that this was an irreversible trend. So the time had come to experiment with main line diesel traction in Great Britain, and the London Midland & Scottish Railway was the first to take the plunge. There was talk of ordering some diesel-electric locomotives from the Electro-Motive Division of General Motors, the USA firm with the most diesel locomotive experience, but eventually it was two British-built diesels, Nos. 10000 and 10001, that emerged from Derby Works nearly at the end of 1947. During 1948 the diesels were mainly on running-in turns between Derby and St. Pancras; then in 1949 they were transferred to the Western Lines, and, working in tandem with multiple-unit control, after operating various trains, they were assigned to the "Royal Scot".

I was myself a passenger on the inaugural down run, when we had a 16-coach load of 545 tons gross, but with 8 hr. 25 min. still allowed for the run from Euston to Glasgow there was little

▲ Revolutionary development in 1947—Britain's first main line diesel-electric locomotives hurry the 16-coach " Royal Scot" through the Lune gorge near Tebay. [J. Hardman]

opportunity for showing what 3,200 hp really could do. At several points, however, particularly when climbing, the diesels were opened out to the point where their performance was superior to anything normally developed by a Stanier steam Pacific. When first introduced, both Nos. 10000 and 10001 were provided with gangway connections of very limited size, and bent double I was able to pass through two of these and so reach the driving cabin. Such connections are standard practice in the United States, where an assemblage of five, six, seven or even more units may head some of the vast freight trains of that country, and ability to pass from unit to unit is almost essential, but this provision on Nos. 10000 and 10001 was never repeated on any later British diesel design.

10 · LMSR Coaching Comfort

At the formation of the group in 1923, London Midland & Scottish coaching stock as a whole was very much a mixed bag. The highest standard in general, probably, was that of the former Midland Railway. Up till 1918 the clerestory roof, first introduced with the Pullman cars imported from America in 1874, had been continued on much Midland main line stock, but at last the more general elliptical type of roof took its place. With the London & North Western Railway clerestories had been confined to dining and sleeping cars; corridor stock had been of a somewhat undistinguished flat-roofed type but had developed through a semi-elliptical stage to the high elliptical roof gradually being standardised by the railways of Britain.

In 1907 the LNWR built a magnificent set of 12-wheel coaches for the special boat trains between Euston and Liverpool, and in the following year turned out a similar pair of trains for the afternoon expresses between London and Glasgow. The latter each comprised eight coaches, four for Glasgow, three for Edinburgh and one for Aberdeen, but one each of the Glasgow and Edinburgh portions was an older clerestory-roofed composite restaurant car, which did not enhance the appearance of the train. In Scotland the finest trains in the first decade of the century had been those built by the Caledonian Railway in 1905 and 1906 for the services from Glasgow and Edinburgh to Aberdeen. These were in competition with the trains of the Caledonian's traditional enemy, the North British Railway, but the latter's rolling stock did not attain the same standard. The Caledonian built similar 12-wheel coaches for its Glasgow-Edinburgh and other services.

It should be added that the rolling stock for Anglo-Scottish trains was jointly owned by the English and Scottish partners, though built to the standard designs of the English companies. So the West Coast coaches, joint property of the London & North Western and Caledonian Railways, bore the letters "WCJS", for "West Coast Joint Stock"; the Midland coaches, at first lettered "MSWJS" for "Midland & South Western Joint Stock", later became "M&GSW", Similarly the Midland coaches working through to the North British line were lettered "M&NB". After the grouping, the LNER claimed its share of the latter, which from then on changed its crimson lake colour to the LNER varnished teak.

Main line coaches of the lines in England in general were about 54 ft. long, except restaurant and sleeping cars, which were up to 65 ft. 6 in.; with such lengths 6-wheel bogies were considered to be essential. Some of the earliest vehicles in Britain to be mounted on twelve wheels were the Midland Pullman cars to which reference has been made already; first introduced in 1874, they were still being imported from the United States up to 1902, and all on 6-wheel bogies. They were both sleeping cars, and also "drawing room" cars for

▼ One of the handsome Caledonian trains of 12-wheel "Grampian Corridor" stock introduced in 1905 on the Glasgow and Edinburgh to Aberdeen services.
[BR

▲ Acme of railway travel luxury—the LMSR Royal train passing Bushey en route from Euston to Ballater, for Balmoral, headed by Claughton 4-6-0 No. 5944.

[F. R. Hebron

day trains, but all had vanished by the time the LMSR was formed.

Meantime, however, another LMSR constituent had introduced Pullman cars on an extensive scale, and this was the Caledonian Railway. They were 12-wheelers, 67 ft. 5 in. long, both of the parlour type, commanding supplementary fares, and also Pullman restaurant and buffet cars, accessible to all passengers without supplementary charge. They worked between Glasgow and Aberdeen, Glasgow and Edinburgh, and even between Glasgow and both Moffat and Crieff. In addition there was the beautiful Pullman observation car *Maid of Morven*, which operated in summer over the highly scenic line between Glasgow and Oban. I have a vivid recollection of travelling with a friend in this car one first of June shortly after World War I, the first day of its operation in that year, when we were the only passengers, sitting in luxurious armchairs looking out of the rear window, and being exclusively served with our meals by an attentive staff—the nearest approach to Royal travel that I could ever have imagined! In conjunction with the Highland Railway, the restaurant cars also ran between Perth and Inverness. These Pullmans were still in operation after the formation of the LMSR, and were the only Pullman cars ever possessed by that company.

Mention of Royalty in the last paragraph brings its reminder of the magnificent set of Royal saloons built in 1941 by the London Midland & Scottish Railway at their Wolverton shops. The previous London & North Western Royal train had been the one most frequently used by the Royal Family, especially on their journeys to and from Balmoral. The three new saloons comprised the King's and Queen's cars, each having bedroom, bathroom and lounge compartment with armchairs—a palace on wheels indeed—and a third car with sleeping accommodation for the staff and a power plant supplying current for lighting and heating. All three cars are carried on 6-wheel bogies, and the two Royal cars are the heaviest passenger vehicles that have ever run on British rails, 57 tons apiece; the staff and power car weighs 52 tons. The reason for building a train of such luxury in wartime was that King George VI and Queen Elizabeth, tireless in mixing with their subjects all round the country, wanted to relieve country houses and others from the difficulty of entertaining them in wartime conditions, and thus elected whenever possible to sleep in the Royal train.

It is interesting to recall that after the formation of the London Midland & Scottish Railway, and the decision to choose Midland red as the standard coach colour, the reigning monarch, King George V, strongly objected to the previous Royal train being divested of its West Coast colours of chocolate and white, and those colours therefore remained. Midland red for coaches and locomotives was another mark of "Midlandisation" in early LMSR days; it meant the disappearance of LNWR and Caledonian chocolate-and-white, Lancashire & Yorkshire brown in two shades, and

▲ A typical Midland coach—12-wheel "dining carriage" built at Derby for the St. Pancras–Glasgow service and lettered M&GSW. [P. J. Sharpe

▼ A standard LMSR third class corridor coach. [BR

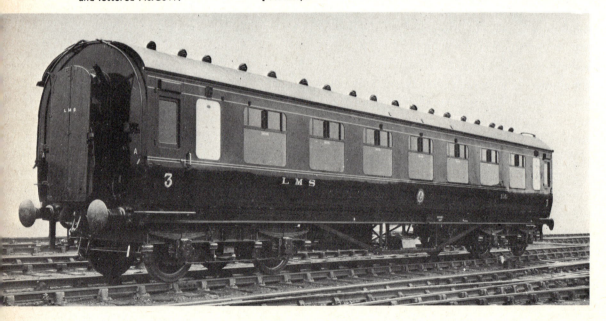

▲ Interior of first class LMSR restaurant car.   [BR   ▼ One of the earliest British buffet cars, showing serving counter and seating area.   [BR

Furness blue and white. Glasgow & South Western and North Staffordshire coaching stock already was painted a crimson lake colour. With LMSR men at the head of rolling stock affairs after nationalisation, it was not surprising that for a number of years Midland red became the standard colour for British Railways coaches also.

After the formation of the LMSR it was not only the Midland coach colour that was standardised, but also in general Midland coach design; this again was not surprising, seeing that R. W. Reid, the Midland Railway Carriage Superintendent, had been appointed Chief Carriage and Wagon Superintendent for the new group. What *was* surprising, however, was that at first, though all-steel coach construction was being adopted on other lines, the LMSR decided to stick to wooden coach-bodies, though on steel underframes. One reason, no doubt, was that the coach works at Derby had by then evolved an efficient mass production system of wooden body building. The only change of importance in Derby design was

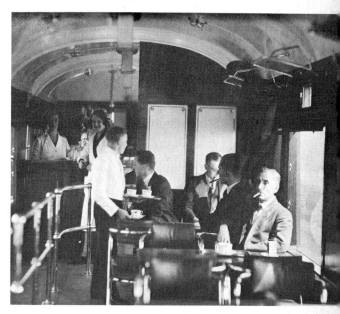

that the standard Midland 54 ft. coach-body length was changed to the London & North Western 57 ft.

The year 1924 saw the building of the pioneer open third-class coaches, which later were to become so popular, with entrance and exit doors at the ends only; but not until 1927 did compartment coaches with end doors only, in this case first class, make their appearance. All coaches were carried on 4-wheel bogies, except dining and sleeping cars, which with lengths gradually increasing to 69 ft. were still being built as 12-wheelers. In 1928 the privilege of sleeping accommodation was extended for the first time to the third class passenger, in 60-ft. coaches with seven compartments, each with four berths; the upper berths were designed to fold back into the compartment walls when out of service, so converting each compartment to ordinary daytime use.

Unlike the LNER, during most of its history the LMSR did not build special train sets for specific services, with furnishing and *décor* superior to that of the general run of the main line stock, but some well-known LMSR expresses certainly had a distinctive character. Until well into the century the Midland Railway, renowned for its restaurant services, had built trains without any corridors linking their cars with the coaches in the rest of the trains in which they ran, expecting passengers requiring meals to ride throughout in the restaurant cars themselves. On certain LMSR business expresses in later years, particularly those between Euston, Liverpool and Manchester, although vestibuled throughout the same practice developed on a considerable scale through the years, until such a train as the Euston-Manchester "Lancastrian" carried an independent kitchen car flanked by two open firsts and two open thirds, all used to capacity during the service of meals.

One pair of special trains, however, was put into service in 1930. It was the challenge of the new trains which the LNER had built for their "Flying Scotsman" in 1928, when non-stop running began between Kings Cross and Edinburgh, that spurred the LMSR to this step, for their 14-coach trains were to be used on the "Royal Scot" service. They did not try to emulate the LNER with cocktail bars or hairdressing rooms, but there were changes, especially in the first class, which included some new semi-open firsts, half compartments and half open seating for meals, and also lounge brakes, the passenger portions of which were open saloons furnished with armchairs and occasional tables.

▶ A Royal Mail van, showing the mail pouches extended outwards for delivery at both ends, and the net opened for collection.   [Postmaster-General

Rather curiously, these latter did not attract the travelling public, and at times I found to my advantage that I could retire to one and use my portable typewriter to my heart's content without disturbing other passengers. At other times the first class *coupé* compartments that were included in many LMSR trains at that time were of the greatest value for the same reason!

It was disappointing that when the "Coronation Scot" started to run in 1937, by comparison with the two unique train sets which Gresley had built for the LNER "Coronation", the LMSR contented itself with two nine-coach sets of standard stock, distinguished only by slightly superior internal fittings, and a blue-and-white exterior in place of the normal Midland red. But in 1939, when the LMSR was preparing to be represented by a locomotive and train at the New York World's Fair, it was a different matter. A magnificent new "Coronation Scot" train was turned out, the first class accommodation including a combined lounge and cocktail bar and a separate club saloon, pressure heating and ventilation, telephones from the compartments to the restaurant car staff, and other novelties. The train was duly shipped to the United States, where it was much admired, but while it was still there the 1939–1945 war broke out. Notwithstanding submarine risks, the locomotive "Coronation" was brought back across the Atlantic early in the war, but a similar risk was not thought worth while for the coaches, which remained in the USA as an officers' club until 1946.

Three sets of coaches had been under construction for the "Coronation Scot", and were completed by 1947, but after the war the train was not restored, and these fine vehicles, incidentally articulated in pairs, which could not be comfortably worked into train seating plans, had to be dispersed and used for a variety of more humdrum purposes—a sad end indeed. Apart from these notable train sets, it cannot be said that the London Midland & Scottish authorities were ever as adventurous in the coaching realm as their London & North Eastern rivals on the other side of the country.

▶ Sorting in progress on the "Night TPO Up Special", from Aberdeen and Glasgow to Euston.
                              [Postmaster-General

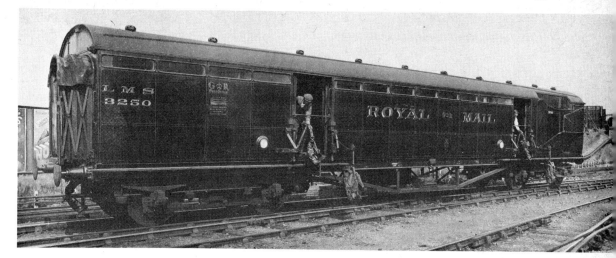

11 · Pre-LMS Passenger Train Services

BETWEEN THE methods of operation of the principal constituents of the LMSR group there were very considerable differences. Over the principal main line of the LNWR between Euston and Crewe, with no gradients steeper than 1 in 330 for most of its length, heavy trains were the rule. Liverpool and Manchester portions, each with their own restaurant cars, were combined during the off-peak hours, and as the double-heading which had been rife during the Webb compound regime had largely ceased, the George the Fifth 4-4-0s and Prince of Wales 4-6-0s had to be thrashed pretty hard to keep time on schedules demanding average speeds up to 55 mph. Even the advent of the more powerful Claughton 4-6-0s from 1913 onwards had not improved the position to any marked extent, and still less the extensive importation of Midland compound 4-4-0s after the formation of the LMSR group.

The Midland Railway, on the other hand, specialised in express trains with strictly limited loads; with all the principal expresses the Class 4 compounds were not permitted to haul more than 260 tons (a maximum of eight coaches); Class 3 4-4-0s were tied down to 220 tons; the smaller Class 2 4-4-0s to 200 tons; and the Class 1 2-4-0s and 4-2-2s to a modest 170 tons (five coaches) only. With one or two of the fastest expresses the limits were no more than 240, 200, 180, and 150 tons respectively. With any heavier loads than these drivers could demand pilot assistance, which was freely given, and found plenty of employment for the remaining 4-2-2s and for some of the numerous 2-4-0s. So widespread was this double-heading that many of the larger 4-4-0s in later years were

fitted with shields below the front buffer-beams to protect their motion from the rush of water when the leading engine of a double-headed train was taking water from track-troughs.

As to Midland freight working, and especially of coal trains, double-heading was the rule rather than the exception until some relief was given from 1928 to 1930 onwards by the introduction of 33 Garratt articulated 2-6-6-2 engines. It is remarkable that this small engine policy, which because of the duplication of engine-crews and locomotive maintenance involved must have been anything but economic, was allowed to persist, not only through Midland history, but through some years of that of the London Midland & Scottish Railway also.

In Scotland McIntosh of the Caledonian Railway had introduced both 4-6-0 engines of considerable power for the principal passenger workings and 0-8-0s for freight, which could handle their duties without assistance, except on the steepest gradients, such as the southern climb to Beattock Summit, up which practically every northbound train had to be banked. Assistance was even more necessary up the lengthy and arduous climbs of the Highland main line; even with the various Highland 4-6-0 types it was impossible to avoid piloting, especially of the night sleeping car trains, which might incorporate in one train formation sleeping cars and through coaches from and to the West Coast, East Coast and

▼ A typical Midland express—Johnson Class 3 4-4-0 No. 714 heads the 1.30 pm from St. Pancras past Mill Hill, with two coaches for Edinburgh and a five-coach set for Glasgow.　　　　　　　　　[F. E. Mackay

Midland routes to London, not to mention Highland stock—a truly marvellous collection of varied rolling stock colours.

We come now to the matter of speed. Over many years there had been no great variation in London & North Western speeds. Up to World War I, as previously mentioned, apart from the principal up morning and down evening services, London-Liverpool and London-Manchester trains were combined between Euston and Crewe, if non-stop taking about 2 hr. 55 min. for this 158 miles. The 6.5 pm from Euston to Manchester and the 9.45 am up, the fastest trains of the day, were allowed 3½ hr.; 3 hr. 35 min., by the 5.55 pm from Euston, was the best time to Liverpool, non-stop over the 192 miles to Edge Hill. Birmingham had

its four 2-hr. non-stop trains to and from Euston, first introduced in 1905 (one up two-hour express had been running since 1902), but Coventry as yet enjoyed little more than connections from Rugby. But by 1914 the LNWR had introduced slip coaches which could be vestibuled to their trains up to the moment of slipping; so Coventry had the use of these on the 11.50 am and 6.55 pm down, with the privilege of access to the restaurant cars en route.

One interesting experiment, from February, 1910 (in anticipation of the inauguration of the new GWR Paddington-Birmingham 2-hr. service via Bicester), was an express from Birmingham at 8.20 am to Broad Street terminus in London, calling at Coventry and Willesden and taking 2¼ hr.

▲ A Precursor 4-4-0 pilots an Experiment 4-6-0 up Camden bank with the 2 pm Corridor to Glasgow and Edinburgh.

▼ A Prince of Wales 4-6-0 with a down London & North Western express of very mixed rolling stock near Hatch End.
[LPC

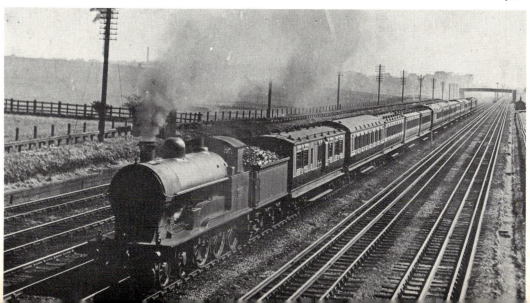

for the run. The return working was at 5.25 pm from Broad Street. It was certainly a novel experience, which I sampled, to get into a restaurant car at this terminus, and to be taking tea as the four-coach train made its way through Dalston Junction and Camden Town before reaching the main line at Chalk Farm. Christened the "City-to-City Express", this was possibly the first true "Inter-City" service in the country, but it failed to attract the city commuters away from Euston, and disappeared in 1914. It may be added that the Willesden Junction stop of this train was common to many expresses right up to World War I.

Mention of long-distance commuters brings its reminder of the provision that was made for some of them who travelled daily from the Lancashire and North Wales coast resorts into Manchester. It was in 1895 that a number of season-ticket holders living in and around Blackpool approached the management of the Lancashire & Yorkshire Railway with an unusual request. If they could guarantee a certain minimum number of first-class season tickets between Blackpool and Manchester, at a higher than the normal rate, would the L&YR provide them with one or two special saloons in place of the compartment stock in which they normally travelled? The proposal was agreed, and shortly afterwards the 5.10 pm from Manchester and the corresponding up morning train were equipped with a couple of "club" saloons, later increased to three, including an attendant and provision for serving refreshments. In the saloons strict rules were observed, each club member having his recognised seat and all strangers being rigidly excluded. The entire trains themselves later became composed of the latest corridor stock, and the same privilege was extended to the corresponding Manchester-Southport expresses. Also in later years similar club saloons were run between Manchester and both Llandudno and Windermere, but all such facilities came to an end with World War I.

The Midland Railway, with its relatively light trains, had always maintained a high standard of speed over its heavily-graded main lines. It was rather amusing, after the 1895 Race to Aberdeen, that nervous passengers between London and Scotland tended to choose the Midland route, thinking that because of the latter's longer times they might travel more safely, but not realising that maximum Midland speeds in general, over some of its lengthy down-grades, were higher than those of either the West or East Coast Routes. Competition with the LNWR had built up a fast service between St. Pancras and Manchester, while Sheffield, Leeds and Bradford all benefited by competition with the Great Northern and the Great Central Railways. Up to World War I

▼ The evening North London "flier" from Broad Street, non-stop with commuters over the LNER main line from Finsbury Park to New Barnet, an archaic collection indeed of rolling stock.

[F. R. Hebron

pitfall slacks in the mining areas between Trent and Chesterfield, and between Rotherham and Normanton, had not begun to bedevil the running over these sections, and the Midland was able to put up some quite respectable times over this main line.

In particular there were various non-stop runs of considerable length, some of them exceeding anything that the LNWR could show in its time-tables. Throughout the year the 1 pm up from Leeds was booked non-stop over the 162 miles from Rotherham to St. Pancras in 180 min. In summer the 10.30 am from Edinburgh to St. Pancras ran through independently, and had no intermediate stop south of Leeds; the time for the 196 miles from Leeds to London at one time came down to 3 hr 33 min., but later was stabilised at 3 hr. 40 min. Longer still was the non-stop break of the summer 11.50 am from St. Pancras to Glasgow, which the Midland rather mendaciously advertised as with "no stop south of the Border", whereas actually there were two such stops, one for passenger purposes at Carlisle, still well clear of the Border, and the other for change of engines on Shipley curve. Even so, the non-stop break of 207 miles from St. Pancras to Shipley was a notable achievement.

▼ One of the toughest of all London suburban loco-motive assignments—London Tilbury & Southend 4-4-2 tank No. 80, with a 13-coach Fenchurch Street to Southend-on-Sea commuter train.

There were similar non-stop runs of note on the Manchester main line. At various periods, in competition with the LNWR, non-stop runs to St. Pancras were scheduled up from both Cheadle Heath and Chinley, of 181¼ and 169½ miles respectively. But the most astonishing effort of this kind was that achieved by an evening express which was introduced on Fridays only from St. Pancras to Liverpool, designed to attract week-end custom to the newly-opened Midland Adelphi Hotel in Liverpool. Leaving London at 6.10 pm, this train arrived in Liverpool Central at 10.20 pm, after having covered a distance of 217¾ miles non-stop, avoiding Derby by the Chaddesden loop, and proceeding from Cheadle Heath by the Cheshire Lines through Timperley to join the CLC main line at Glazebrook. One cannot help thinking that engine-crews on this train at times must have had some anxieties about water, with no chance of taking any more after the track-troughs at Hathern, 105 miles from their destination, and with the Peak Forest summit to be tackled in between.

In Scotland the Caledonian Railway had a few smart timings. In particular the southbound "West Coast Postal" distinguished itself for some years by being booked over the level 32½ miles from Forfar to Perth in 32 min., with load limited to six coaches; northbound, with an even more limited four coaches, the same train had to run the 89¾ miles from Perth to Aberdeen in 97 min. Between Carlisle and Glasgow up to 1932 the

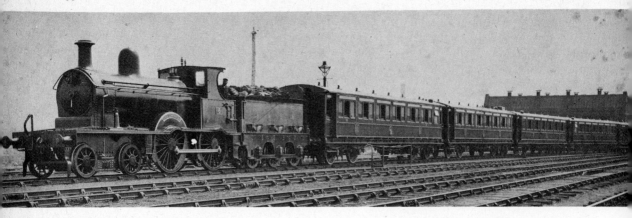

▲ On the Northern Counties Committee line in Ireland—2-cylinder compound 4-4-0 No. 3 *King Edward VII* with a five-coach Belfast–Portrush express.

▼ Not very flattering to the LNWR—one of its 5 ft. 3 in. gauge trains on the Dundalk, Newry & Greenore line, with 0-6-0 saddle tank No. 5.   [LPC

West-East Coast agreement on day train times was a restraining influence, but the fastest night sleeping car train, the 8-hr. 11.50 pm from London Euston, had a non-stop booking of 125 min. for the $102\frac{1}{2}$ miles, which for the period was not bad going. The "Corridor"—2 pm from Euston—was allowed 127 min. for the same distance, including a stop at Strawfrank Junction, Carstairs, to detach the Edinburgh portion.

Between Carlisle and Glasgow the Glasgow & South Western Railway had to work one night and three day trains from St. Pancras, the latter leaving London at 9.30 and 11.30 am and 1.30 pm, with their up counterparts at 9.20 and 11 am and 1.30 pm from St. Enoch. Of these the two afternoon expresses were the fastest, taking 2 hr. 22 min. for the Carlisle-Glasgow run with regular stops at Kilmarnock and conditional ones at Dumfries; but these were normally with five-coach loads only, and neither train reappeared after World War I.

A well-known G&SW train that continued into LMSR days was the 5.10 pm express from St. Enoch to Stranraer, non-stop over the $41\frac{1}{4}$ miles to Ayr in 50 min., which by 1939 had come down to 45 min.; by this time also commuters were being served with tea in a palatial restaurant car which was built during R. H. Whitelegg's reign as Chief Mechanical Engineer at Kilmarnock Works.

Over the Highland main line the minimum time for the 118 miles between Perth and Inverness was $3\frac{1}{4}$ hr., and the heavier trains, in particular the London sleepers, needed 4 hr. or slightly over; one or two trains took the original route by way of Forres and Nairn rather than the direct line between Aviemore and Inverness. On Thursdays only in summer the "Further North Express" ran from Wick to Inverness in 4 hr. 50 min., returning at 4.35 pm on Fridays on a $4\frac{3}{4}$-hr. run; but with other trains a wearisome $6\frac{3}{4}$ to 7 hr. was needed for this last 161-mile journey.

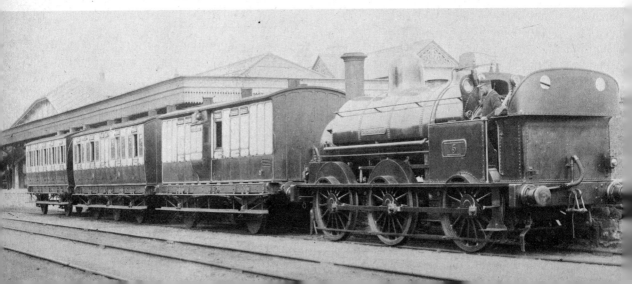

12 · *LMSR Timetable Development*

ON THE formation of the London Midland & Scottish Railway in 1923 the railways of Britain had more or less recovered from their arrears of maintenance and shortage of rolling stock after World War I, but as yet improvement of the passenger train services was a slow process. Their publicity departments, however, were seeking new ways of attracting the attention of the public to their wares, and one such, in the years 1927 and 1928, was an outbreak of train naming. It began with the title "Royal Scot", applied to the 10 am from Euston and its 10 am opposite number from Glasgow Central, after the new set trains had been introduced with non-stop runs between Euston and Carlisle, and soon spread to the night Anglo-Scottish trains—the "Night Scot" between Euston and Glasgow and the "Royal Highlander" from Euston to Inverness and back. Then followed the day trains by the Midland route, the "Thames-Forth Express" between St. Pancras and Edinburgh, and the "Thames-Clyde Express" between St. Pancras and Glasgow St. Enoch.

Many of the principal trains south of the Border were taken in hand in the same way. The 9.45 am from Liverpool to Euston and its return working at 5.55 pm became the "London-Merseyside Express" (later altered to the shorter "Merseyside Express"); the corresponding Manchester trains at 9.45 am up and 6 pm down were christened the "Mancunian", soon after changed in the latter case to the "Lancastrian", running up from Manchester at noon. The boat train from Euston to Fleetwood and later to Heysham was named the "Ulsterman", and the summer expresses to North Wales and the Lake District the "Welshman" and the "Lakes Express" respectively. The direct express which the LMSR had put on in 1925 between St. Pancras and Bradford, avoiding Leeds by using the Royston and Thornhill line, became the "Yorkshireman". Not until 1938 did any Midland trains between St. Pancras and Manchester acquire names; two of these then were named the "Peak Express" and the "Palatine" respectively.

From 1905 there had been in existence the "Sunny South Express", running daily between Liverpool, Manchester, Brighton and Eastbourne, and later extended to Hastings and with a through portion from Birmingham; but with the spread of the family motorcar this had become a week-end service only by the end of LMSR days. In 1910,

also, the competing LNWR and Midland Companies had combined to introduce a through "Pines Express" between Liverpool, Manchester and Bournemouth, transferred from one railway to the other at New Street, Birmingham, and finishing from Bath over the Somerset & Dorset Joint Line. Another cross-country service in which the Midland Railway joined forces with the Great Western was the "Devonian" from Bradford and Leeds, via Derby and Bristol, to Torquay and Paignton. This express received its distinctive name in 1927.

Not until nine years after the grouping did the LMSR management at last come to the realisation that higher speeds were being urgently called for. With the advent of the Royal Scot and Patriot 4-6-0s more adequate passenger power was now available, and with Stanier having just succeeded to the post of Chief Mechanical Engineer a much greater accession of power was in prospect. Finally, the termination of the long-standing West Coast-East Coast agreement not to cut the times of the day Anglo-Scottish trains had opened the door wide to acceleration of these most important services, and if so, why should not the other main line services follow suit?

So the two new LMSR timetable issues in May and October, 1932, contained some revolutionary changes. The "Royal Scot" $8\frac{1}{4}$-hr. timing from Euston was cut at one stroke by 35 min. to Glasgow and 30 min. to Edinburgh. From Liverpool the 5.20 pm express for the first time brought this Merseyside city within 3 hr. 20 min. of London, a timing which involved covering the 152.7 miles from Crewe to Willesden Junction in 142 min., at a start-to-stop average of 64.5 mph. The up "Mancunian", at 9.45 am from Manchester, was given a timing of 172 min over the 176.9 miles from Wilmslow to Euston, while the 5.40 pm up from Manchester, covering the 133.4 miles from Stafford to Euston in 127 min., and with a 40-min. acceleration overall, joined the 9.45 am up and the 6 pm down "Lancastrian" in cutting the Euston-Manchester time to $3\frac{1}{4}$ hr. The up evening express was now named the "Comet"; in the down direction this name was carried by the 11.50 am from Euston to Liverpool and Manchester, with accelerations of 20 min. to both cities. Many expresses were speeded up by 15 to 20 min.

The same thing happened on the Midland Division. By now timings of 105 min. in each

▲ An exceptional power combination—two Claughton 4-6-0s rebuilt with Caprotti valves and large boilers, Nos. 5908 and 5981, lift the down "Lancastrian" up Camden Bank out of Euston. [F. R. Hebron

▼ Improvisation for peak traffic—Claughton 4-6-0 No. 207 *Sir Charles Cust* has the humble task of hauling four-wheel North London suburban stock from Euston to Wembley for a Cup Final. [F. R. Hebron

direction had reappeared over the 99 miles between St. Pancras and Leicester, and there were 75 min. bookings over the 72 miles between St. Pancras and Kettering. The 4.55 pm "Yorkshireman" from St. Pancras was brought down to a time of 3 hr. 2 min. to Sheffield, and the 6.15 pm, non-stop over the 119.7 miles to Trent in 129 min., now reached Leeds in 3 hr. 49 min. As to the Midland "Scotsmen", the "Thames-Clyde" and "Thames-Forth" expresses were both 20 min. faster; the 11.45 am from St. Pancras to Glasgow, altered to start at 12 noon, had to run the 69.8 miles from Luton to Leicester in 72 min. In addition to those already mentioned, several bookings at over a mile-a-minute from start to stop now appeared in the LMSR timetables.

After this substantial speed-up, matters continued without much change until 1936, when the "Midday Scot" was taken in hand. In the 1932 accelerations the Euston-Glasgow time of this express had been cut from 8½ hr. to 8 hr. 5 min.;

now came a reversion from a 1.30 pm departure to the historic 2 pm, and a cut of another 25 min. to 7 hr. 35 min. overall, 5 min. faster than the "Royal Scot". But this was merely the curtain-raiser to the introduction in the following year, 1937, of the 6½ hr. "Coronation Scot". From the same date the up "Midday Scot", following the "Coronation Scot" 5 min. later out of Glasgow Central, picked up en route portions from Aberdeen at Law Junction, Edinburgh at Symington, and (in summer) from Stranraer at Carlisle, so becoming a very weighty train of up to 14 or 15 coaches, but with all stops taking no more than 7 hr. 55 min. to Euston.

On the Caledonian section the Anglo-Scottish accelerations resulted in considerably faster running between Carlisle and Glasgow. The 9-coach "Coronation Scot" had to cover the 102.3 miles each way in 105 min.; and there was a run over the 67 miles from Symington to Carlisle in 69 min. The times of the principal trains between Glasgow and Aberdeen had been steadily coming down, and in 1938, with the help of Stanier's 3-cylinder Jubilee 4-6-0s, for the first time in history two expresses daily were put on to 3-hr. schedules

▼ No longer permitted on express passenger trains—two 4-wheel horseboxes on a down LNWR express, headed by George the Fifth 4-4-0 No. 5000 *Coronation*.
[F. R. Hebron

between these cities, calling only at Perth and at Forfar or Stonehaven. At the same time the former names of "Bon Accord", "Grampian", "Granite City" and "St. Mungo", dating back to the introduction of the palatial "Grampian Corridor" stock in 1905, were restored.

The Jubilee 4-6-0s had also made possible substantial improvements in the service between Euston, Coventry, Birmingham and Wolverhampton. In October, 1935, the LMSR assumed a lead over the Great Western Railway which the latter never afterwards regained or even equalled. The LMSR 4-6-0s had sufficient power to cover the 113 miles of the LMSR route in 115 min. inclusive of a stop at Coventry; four down and three up expresses did so daily. Three down and three up trains took the even 2-hr., one of these including two intermediate stops, and another—the 6.20 pm from Birmingham—no fewer than three stops, at Coventry, Rugby and Watford, which required a booked time of 60 min. for the 65 miles from Rugby to Watford Junction start to stop. The Watford stop was made by several down morning and up evening expresses, for the benefit of passengers from or to the north-western suburbs of London; during World War II period practically every main line train eventually called at Watford, and since the electrification this has now become standard practice with the great majority of down expresses in the morning peak period and their counterparts coming up in the evening.

In 1938 the LMSR operating authorities considered that the time had come to attempt some relief of the Western Division Euston-Manchester service by making more use of their Midland route. In the former days of fierce competition between the London & North Western and the Midland for this traffic, the Midland, despite their far steeper gradients and 980 ft. Peak Forest summit, had got as near to the fastest LNWR time of 3½ hr. as 3 hr. 35–40 min. In later Midland days the down Manchester service had been re-organised on an even-interval basis, with the expresses leaving the terminus at 25 min. past the hour, which earned for them the nickname of "The Twenty-fives"; in 1938 the starting times were altered to 30 min. past.

The 10.30 am down became the "Peak Express", and restored the former 3 hr. 35 min. time; the 10 am up "Palatine" took 3 hr. 48 min., and the 4.25 pm up "Peak Forest" 3 hr. 47 min.; while the down "Palatine", at 4.30 pm from St. Pancras, was slower, with more stops and an overall time of

▲ Part of the burrowing junction complex at Camden—the local lines as seen from an express on the up fast line. [M. S. Welch

3 hr. 56 min. Six-coach train sets were used, with one to two "extras" over parts of the journeys, but there is no record of this enterprise having diverted much traffic from the former rival route. Who could have foreseen that during the electrification of the Western Division main line, apart from one or two morning and evening trains, the Midland route would become the *only* means of rail communication between London and Manchester, whereas now, with the electric service in operation, there is no direct Midland main line still in existence.

In the last years before World War II 60 mph had become a recognised standard of speed which could be used for publicity purposes. For this I may have been indirectly responsible, because for some years I had been conducting an annual article in the *Railway Magazine*, under the *nom-de-plume* "Mercury", listing all the British runs exceeding in speed 58 mph from start to stop. By 1938 and 1939 the LMSR was paring many of its running times so as to bring them just within the mile-a-minute limit, and thus to increase their aggregate mileage so timed. Eventually, though the LMSR was unable to claim the fastest runs, it certainly could boast by far the greatest

▲ Parcels trains form an important part of passenger operation. One such from Holyhead passes Conway Castle, with Class 5 4-6-0 No. 45003 in charge.
[Derek Cross

▼ Engine headboards for a time adorned the principal named trains. Here Pacific No. 6240 *City of Coventry* carries the handsome headdress of the "Royal Scot" as it climbs past Greskine on Beattock Bank.
[Eric Treacy

aggregate mile-a-minute mileage. This amounted to 28 runs totalling 6,902 miles, as compared with 24 runs (2,187 miles) on the Great Western, 23 runs (2,896 miles) on the London & North Eastern, and none on the Southern.

Many of the LMSR runs just scraped within the 60 mph limit, such as the "Royal Scot's" 299 min. for the 299.1 miles from Euston to Carlisle, four 123-min. Midland runs over the 123.5 miles between St. Pancras and Nottingham, and eleven 99 min. runs over the 99.1 miles between St. Pancras and Leicester, with others too numerous to mention. It was only in the higher ranges of speed that the LNER had the supremacy, with 6 runs of 1,293 miles in length timed at over 64 mph compared with the LMSR two of 223 miles, and six at from 67.9 to 71.9 mph as against nothing as fast on the LMSR.

One further feature of note of this period was the LMSR "On Time" campaign, fostered by every possible means, and wherever possible competitively. There is no question that this campaign had a considerable effect on locomotive crews, locomotive maintenance at depots, and also on station staffs, signalmen, guards and all others concerned with operation, and so helped to raise the *esprit de corps* of the staff as a whole. We might well benefit by a similar enterprise in these days of British Rail. Little further needs to be said about the LMSR between 1939 and the end of the Company's history in 1947. The effect of World War II on train services was even worse than in World War I, and included much severe damage to railway property, so that train services were far from back to their pre-war standard when nationalisation took effect in 1948.

▼ Hilton Junction, south of Perth, where the main Caledonian line from Stirling was joined (left) by the North British from Edinburgh (now closed).
[K. R. Pirt

▶ One of the ubiquitous Midland standard 0-6-0 engines works a mixed freight train past Cheltenham.
[Derek Cross

13 · *Freight, Marshalling and Centralised Control*

OF THE various constituent companies which went to form the London Midland & Scottish, the Midland undoubtedly took the lead in the freight realm. In the heart of its territory were the coalfields of Leicestershire, Nottinghamshire, Derbyshire and South Yorkshire, all disgorging their loads of coal which were distributed in all directions by the Midland. To carry out this and other freight services, just before the beginning of World War I, the Midland Railway in 1914 possessed no fewer than 100,622 open and mineral wagons, as compared with 53,353 only owned by the London & North Western; the nearest approach to the Midland total was the 93,708 open and mineral wagons of the North Eastern and 55,338 of the Great Western. These numbers were, of course, additional to covered, cattle and other wagons, not to mention the numerous private owners' wagons. A significant Midland figure was that out of the total of 71,005,580 engine miles run by MR locomotives in 1914, no fewer than 6,820,695 were "assisting, light, etc." miles—a startling evidence of the effect to which MR engine mileage was increased by double-heading.

In the freight realm, however, the Midland could claim one important development that was to have far-reaching results. It began in 1907 when a traffic inspector from the Derby district, named J. H. Follows, was transferred to the staff of the newly appointed General Superintendent, Cecil Paget, and was posted to take charge of a freight office at Masborough, just north of Sheffield. Here he began to investigate the long hours of freight train staffs, and with such success that by 1911 what at the time of his appointment had averaged 20,000 hours of unreasonably long hours of duty had been completely eliminated. This achievement so impressed Paget that as early as 1908 he had not only had the Masborough office equipped telephonically and in other ways to deal with the whole matter of train control, but by 1909 had decided to bring all goods and mineral traffic between Cudworth and Toton under the supervision of district controllers stationed at Cudworth, Staveley, Westhouses and Toton, in addition to Masborough. Finally came the decision to apply freight train control to the whole of the Midland system, with 25 district offices and a Central Control at Derby, the first of its kind in Great Britain.

The work of these offices, of course, went far

▲ Introduced to dispense with double-heading of Midland coal trains between Toton and Cricklewood —2-6-6-2 Garratt No. 47967, with the revolving coal bunker introduced to ease the fireman's work.
[P. H. Wells

▶ Mainstay of heavy London & North Western freight working—a Crewe-built 0-8-0 emerges from a tunnel at Chester. [P. M. Alexander

beyond the mere control of staff hours. It covered the timing and composition of trains, the diagramming of locomotives, the availability of wagons, and every other detail of freight train working. Basic to the scheme were a series of elaborate line diagrams showing in detail all line facilities connected with freight train operation, and track diagrams of all regular freight train paths and all paths available for conditional workings. Locomotives were classified according to their power, and for easy recognition had their numbers painted in large numerals on their tender or tank sides.

Follows was responsible in large measure for working out these plans, and it was entirely appropriate that not only did he work up himself to the position of General Superintendent of the Midland Railway before the end of that company's

history, but that in 1923 he became the first General Superintendent of the London Midland & Scottish Railway. His Midland control system revolutionised freight working on the MR, in punctuality, efficiency and economy, and eventually became the pattern for freight operation over Great Britain generally.

If the Midland Railway led the country in the matter of freight train control, the London & North Western Railway was the first to lay out a freight marshalling yard operated entirely by gravity. There had been one or two limited uses of gravity elsewhere in wagon sorting, but nothing else to equal the marshalling yard installation brought into use in 1875 at Edge Hill, Liverpool, at the complicated point of convergence of the main lines from Crewe and Manchester with those

▲ The Fowler LMSR 0-8-0 design—No. 49582 (BR numbering) getting away from Chinley North Junction with a train of empties for Sheffield.
[T. Lewis

▼ Empties through the mountains—Class 5 4-6-0 No. 45135 with a very neat turn-out of about 50 of them in the Lune gorge near Tebay. [Ivo Peters

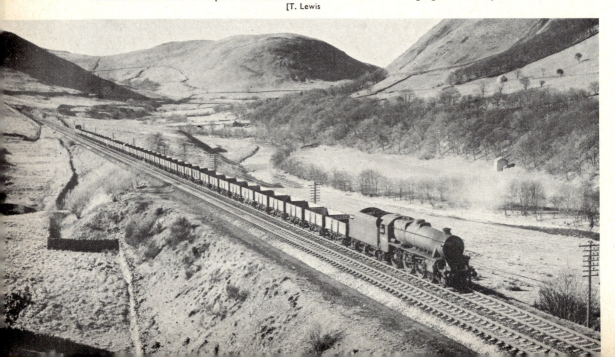

from the various quays and docks on the Mersey.

There was no need to raise any artificial "humps" to provide the necessary gradients, as the marshalling yard was laid out on downward sloping ground with an average inclination of 1 in 93. It was therefore only necessary to draw each train to be marshalled to the upper end of the yard, and then, having uncoupled the wagons, to let each roll by gravity into its appropriate siding in the "gridirons". In those early days, of course, all the switches had to be moved by hand, and many shunters were needed to brake the wagons to prevent violent impacts with the wagons that were already in the sidings; many years were to elapse before marshalling yards would be provided with artificial humps, automatic control of all switching by electric or electronic power, and automatic retarders to brake each wagon to a stop.

The biggest marshalling yard on the LMSR was Toton, on the Erewash Valley main line of the Midland just north of the complex of lines that converge from London, Derby, Nottingham and Burton at Trent Junction. Not until after nationalisation, however, were the whole of the 35 down and 37 up reception sidings brought into use on both sides of the main line to the North, and the hump cabin and "king", "queen" and "jack" points completely mechanised and equipped with retarders. This was in 1939; but the London & North Eastern Railway by 1929 had established a ten-year lead in the complete mechanisation, with retarders, of its great yard at Whitemoor, in Cambridgeshire. This installation was studied by E. J. H. Lemon, who in 1931 had succeeded J. H. Follows as LMSR General Superintendent, and in view of the speeding up and the economies that the Whitemoor scheme had made possible, it is astonishing that not until 1937 were any serious steps taken to deal similarly with Toton, where, as just mentioned, the re-equipment was completed in 1939.

However, Lemon had not been idle in other forms of freight mechanisation during his term of office. In 1933 he engaged a specialist in works reorganisation and industrial matters, Lewis Ord, to investigate the handling of freight at goods and other stations, and report as to how it might be expedited and cheapened. The enquiry began with the great Crewe Tranship Shed, and spread to depots all over the LMSR system, and was directed mainly to recommending how mechanical handling could reduce human effort. It extended to the elimination, where possible, of trucking; reduction of unnecessary walking by staff, exten-

sion of the use of containers and cheaper handling methods, reductions in the use of shunting locomotives by the use of capstans and in other ways, and by such aids the quicker release of wagons under load.

The Ord report was lengthy and drastic. It recommended complete remodelling at various freight depots, and new equipment and changes of handling methods at various others. In 1935 parcels traffic came similarly under review, and resulted, *inter alia*, in the installation of conveyor belts at various centres, especially at Holyhead for the transfer of mails between the ships and the shore. E. J. H. Lemon and J. H. Follows between them thus played a considerable part in expediting the work and reducing the cost of London Midland & Scottish freight handling.

▲ Toton mechanised marshalling yard on the Midland—the control tower and one of the retarders.　[BR

▼ Toton marshalling yard, looking down from the hump past the king, queen and jack points to the fan of marshalling sidings.　[BR

14 · The LMSR On and Across the Water

WITH THE formation of the London Midland & Scottish Railway a considerable amount of maritime activity was brought under one direction. Much of it concerned communication between Great Britain and Ireland. There was the well patronised service between Holyhead and Kingstown (the present Dun Laoghaire), in which the LNWR competed with the City of Dublin Steam Packet Company, with relations between them far from friendly; the latter had the mail contract, which the LMSR in later years succeeded in wresting from them, after which the LMSR had the route to themselves.

From Kingstown the then Dublin, Wicklow & Wexford worked the boat trains into Dublin, with through coaches which were continued by the Great Southern & Western Railway to Cork, the Midland Great Western to Galway and the Great Northern to Belfast. The LNWR also ran its own steamer service to North Wall, in the heart of Dublin, and yet another service to Greenore, from which the Irish Great Northern provided a connecting restaurant car train to Belfast. This Northern Irish city in addition was served more directly by a steamer service from Fleetwood, operated jointly by the London & North Western and Lancashire & Yorkshire Railways.

Then in 1904 the Midland Railway, which up to that date had been running its own steamers to Belfast from Piel Pier and later from the Furness Railway's Ramsden Dock at Barrow, brought into use its own magnificent new harbour at Heysham, adjacent to Morecambe, and established a new steamer service between there and Belfast. Not only so, but in the previous year the Midland had obtained a foothold in Northern Ireland by acquiring the entire system of the Belfast & Northern Counties Railway, from Belfast to Larne, Ballymena, Portrush and Londonderry.

Soon after the London Midland & Scottish Railway had come into being it became clear that so many services across the Irish Sea by the one railway were overdone. Certainly passenger traffic between Holyhead and Greenore had ceased in 1926, and the one remaining ship on this route was carrying freight only, but the ex-LNWR-LYR Fleetwood steamers were still competing with those of the ex-Midland Railway from Heysham. So in 1928 it was decided to abandon the Fleetwood route, and to concentrate on that via Heysham, for which three fine new ships had been ordered.

New connections were laid in at Morecambe between the former LNW and Midland lines, to enable the "Ulster Express" from Euston to be diverted from Fleetwood to Heysham, and with departure from Euston at 6.10 pm, instead of the one-time 5.30 pm to Fleetwood, and a Belfast arrival at 8.0 instead of 9.30 am, over two hours in all were cut from the journey. From St. Pancras the connecting train, with its more lengthy journey, had now to start an hour earlier, at 5.0 pm, but this was continued mainly for the benefit of the intermediate cities, such as Sheffield and Leeds, to which it also gave a fast evening service from London.

Further north in Great Britain another service to Ireland was and still is provided between Stranraer, in the south-west corner of Scotland, and Larne; with half the voyage completed in the sheltered water of Loch Ryan and the open sea crossing beyond being the shortest of any between Great Britain and Ireland this route has always been popular with those who are not good sailors. But a strong north-west wind, sweeping through this narrow channel as through a funnel, can make

▼ The SS *Duke of Lancaster*, one of the fine ships introduced in 1928 on the Heysham-Belfast service.
[BR

this crossing as rough as any round our island. The Stranraer service, with the connecting Portpatrick & Wigtownshire Joint Railway from Castle Douglas, was owned and operated jointly by the London & North Western, Midland, Caledonian and Glasgow & South Western Railways, all constituents of the LMSR.

The biggest fleet that came into LMSR ownership at the grouping, however, was that of the Lancashire & Yorkshire Railway, on the other side of the country, which provided a cargo service between the port of Goole, on the Humber, and a number of different Continental ports; there were some 25 of these LYR ships, in addition to two operated jointly with the North Eastern Railway between Hull and Zeebrugge, another

plying between Liverpool and Drogheda, and the five joint LNWR-LYR ships on the Fleetwood-Belfast run. The port of Liverpool was still the starting-point of ocean liner services to various parts of the world, for which the LNWR provided boat trains from Euston to Liverpool Riverside, but well before 1923 all the principal Transatlantic liners, such as those of the Cunard Line, had transferred themselves to Southampton.

Fifteen years after the acquisition by the Midland Railway of the London Tilbury & Southend line in 1912, the LMSR in 1927 conceived the idea of getting a share of the lucrative traffic between Great Britain and the Continent by establishing a steamer service between Tilbury and Dunkerque in 1927. The steamer *Alsacien* was provided by a

▲ Holyhead Harbour, with SS *Cambria*, on the Holyhead–Dun Laoghaire run. [BR

▼ Turbine propulsion on the Clyde—SS *Caledonia* of the Caledonian Steam Packet Company. [BR

French company; on the English side through coaches were run from various parts of the Midland system by evening trains to Tilbury; passengers slept on board and were brought by the SNCF into Paris by 11.20 am—a somewhat similar service to the SR "Night Ferry", but, of course, without any through sleeping cars. The public does not readily change its travelling habits, however, unless something very attractive is offered, and with the additional handicap of fogs in the Thames, which led to unpunctuality, this experiment was but short-lived.

Finally, among maritime activities in a more limited area, mention must be made of the thriving steamer services on the Clyde, highly popular for residential reasons and also for holiday trips for Glaswegians. Competition was extremely keen between the Caledonian, Glasgow & South Western and North British Railways; the Caledonian services were operated by the independent Caledonian Steam Packet Company. The Caledonian piers were at Gourock and Wemyss Bay, the Glasgow & South Western at Princes Pier (Greenock), Largs and Fairlie, and both railways also ran boat trains to Ardrossan for the steamers to Arran and Belfast.

Incidentally, the two lines to the latter ran parallel for some distance west of Kilwinning, and spirited races between the two companies' boat trains were of frequent occurrence. Times were also cut to a minimum with the services for commuters between Glasgow and Dunoon; here the G&SWR was at a disadvantage with the hefty climbs which its boat trains between St. Enoch and Princes Pier had to surmount to the summit between Kilmacolm and Greenock. The grouping, of course, brought the Caledonian and Glasgow & South Western fleets into common

ownership, and from then on it was case of the LMSR competing with the LNER, as the North British had now become.

A word is now needed about the overseas commitments of the London Midland & Scottish. In Ireland the Northern Counties Committee, as the former Belfast & Northern Counties had been styled after acquisition by the MR in 1903, was a substantial property, with 201 route miles of 5 ft. 3 in. gauge track, and 62 miles of 3 ft. gauge. The Midland also was joint owner with the Irish Great Northern Railway of the County Donegal Railways Joint Committee.

Until well into LMSR days the main Northern Counties line from Belfast to Portrush and Londonderry took off in a trailing direction from the Belfast-Larne line at Greenisland, where all the trains from and to the west had to reverse. An important development by the LMSR, completed in 1934, was the direct spur from Bleach Green Junction to Monkstown that cut out the Greenisland reversal, and made possible some substantial accelerations of the service between Belfast, Portrush and Londonderry. Some massive concrete viaducts were required to carry both the down line and the flyover by which the up line joined the line from Larne.

Owing to the difference in gauge, locomotives and rolling stock for the NCC section in Ireland had to be specially designed and built at Derby, and in anticipation of the accelerated services, some very capable 6 ft. 2-6-0 locomotives were turned out in 1933 to Stanier's designs. The greater than normal space between the coupled

▼ In Northern Ireland. Northern Counties Committee 2-6-0 No. 103 *Thomas Somerset* with a 5 ft. 3 in. gauge Belfast–Portrush train at Dunloy.
[J. Macartney Robbins

▲ Sent to represent Great Britain at the Chicago Exhibition in 1893 and worked a train from Chicago to New York—Webb 2-2-2-2 3-cylinder compound No. 2054 *Queen Empress* of the LNWR, specially painted white and with the Royal arms.　　[BR

▼ With American bell and headlight, LMSR 4-6-0 No. 6100 *Royal Scot* represented Great Britain at the Chicago "Century of Progress Exposition" in 1933, and worked its train across the USA from the Atlantic to the Pacific and back.　　[H. W. Pontin

wheels made it possible both to lower the pitch of the boilers above rail, and also to increase the size of the fireboxes, so that these were more capable machines than their modest appearance might have suggested. A new train called the "North Atlantic Express" put Portrush within 75 min. of Belfast.

It should be added that the former London & North Western Railway also had two modest possessions on Irish soil, which came into LMSR ownership at the grouping. One was in Dublin, connecting its North Wall quay with the Great Northern and Midland Great Western Railways; the other was the 26-mile Dundalk, Newry & Greenore Railway, which provided a connection from its Greenore steamers to both Dundalk and Newry. But the ancient 0-6-0 saddle tanks and 6-wheel coaches which provided the DNGR

passenger service hardly reflected any glory upon their English owners!

Reference needs to be made finally to two further LMSR overseas activities, one of which took one of the company's locomotives as far away from home as the Pacific coast of the United States. Spurred on by the successful visit in 1927 of the Great Western Railway's 4-6-0 *King George V* to the "Fair of the Iron Horse" in Baltimore, the LMSR decided to be represented similarly at the "Century of Progress Exposition" in Chicago in 1933. This was a considerably more ambitious plan, as it required running for many hundreds of miles over American tracks, and eventually involved a tour of no less than 11,194 miles. The engine sent over carried the number 6100 and name *Royal Scot* (although actually another engine of the same class was substituted) with seven "Royal Scot" coaches and a sleeping car. All were transported across the Atlantic to Montreal, from which city a circuitous journey of 3,181 miles was made to Chicago.

So great was the interest of the Americans, however, that after the exhibition had closed it was decided to give a much wider American public the chance of seeing the stranger in action. So the *Royal Scot* and train ran westwards from Chicago to Los Angeles, then up the Pacific coast to San Francisco and across the Canadian frontier to Vancouver, and finally by the Canadian Pacific main line through the Rockies and back to Montreal and home. During this extensive tour no fewer than 3,021,601 Canadians and Americans passed through the train. It was greatly to the credit of British locomotive building that throughout this strenuous circuit, using American coal and negotiating some long and steep climbs through the mountains (to a maximum altitude of 7,242 ft.), the British engine suffered not one single mechanical failure.

Six years later an even greater "World's Fair" at New York once again proved a lure to the LMSR, and it was decided to boost Great Britain by exhibiting a train of the latest type. This time Stanier, who had only just assumed office at the time of *Royal Scot*'s expedition, was able to send one of his latest streamlined Pacifics to represent the country. It bore the number and name 6220 *Coronation*, but was actually No. 6229 *Duchess of Hamilton*, which had been more recently overhauled. As with the *Royal Scot*, the engine had to be fitted with the headlight and bell required by American law for running over American tracks. This time, unhappily, the trip was not so fortuitous, for before the end of the exhibition World War II had broken out. Braving the risks of submarine attack, the locomotive was shipped back to England early in the war, but it was not until after the end of the war that the coaches followed suit. While the World's Fair lasted, however, Americans were certainly given an impressive demonstration of the best in British rail travel.

▼ Next visitor to the USA in 1939, was the streamlined Stanier Pacific No. 6220 *Coronation*, with a new "Coronation Scot" train, seen here at work on the Baltimore & Ohio main line.   [H. W. Pontin